MW00874696

Sunflower Wisdom

Find & Follow the Light in Your Life

Felicia Brown

Other Titles and Products by Felicia Brown

BOOKS IN ENGLISH

Free & Easy Ways to Promote Your Massage, Spa & Wellness Business
Creating Lifetime Clients: How to WOW Your Customers for Life
Every Touch Marketing: Free & Easy Ways to Promote Yourself or Your Small Business
Reflections of My Heart: A Poetic Journey of Love, Life, Heartbreak & Healing
The Sunflower Princess: A Healing Fairy Tale
Wisdom of the Stone
Contributing Author of *Thank God I…Volume 3*

LIBROS EN ESPAÑOL

Every Touch Marketing: Maneras Gratuitas y Sencillas de Promocionar su Negocio de Masaje, Spa y Bienestar
Clientes Para Toda La Vida: Cómo Impresionar a sus Clientes Para Siempre
La Princesa del Girasol: Un Cuento de Hadas para Sanarte

E-BOOKS

How to Get New Clients
Getting Clients to Rebook
Upselling and Upgrading
Retailing for Massage, Spa & Salon Pros
Successful Event Planning Guide

HOME STUDY PROGRAMS

Smart Spa Marketing
Every Touch Marketing 6 Week Home Study Course
Every Touch Marketing 12 Week Intensive Home Study Course

CDs

Goal Setting: Create Success for Your Life and Business
Just Breathe: Guided Meditations for Inner Peace

Deep in their roots, all flowers keep the light.

Theodore Roethke

DEDICATION

To my grandparents, Pearle and Ernest Wood....

Thank you for teaching me to be persistent and true to myself. I am so incredibly lucky I got to be the unexpected "light" in your life and to have had you as mine. I know you both watch over me to this day and believe you would be proud of the woman I have become. You continue to inspire me to do and be my best. I love you both forever.

CONTENTS

Introduction

The following pages contain a collection of personal musings and essays written to explore the curiosities of my life. As both a seeker and (over) thinker, I tend to look not only for the meaning contained inside the events I experience, but also the hidden lessons, wisdom and gifts.

I'm not sure when I started this practice but have been writing about my life since I was a pre-teen, perhaps after I was first given a diary. My grandmother always kept a daily diary to make note of significant events and to keep track of appointments. Though she did not fill the pages of her mini-journals with the same kinds of ramblings I have, I think her habit might be what started mine.

For me, and perhaps in general, I think journaling itself eventually gives way to reflection and introspection, particularly if you are prone to re-reading what you've committed to the page. Certainly, writing these personal notes as well as more public blogs and articles has been a tool for my own growth and healing. This has been especially helpful as a means to look backward to see "where I was" in the past and measure (hopefully) how far I've progressed forward since those words were written.

Writing is also a way for me to process all the half-formed thoughts floating between my ears and bouncing off the neurons. Sometimes, as I take the time to get everything down, to sort details and remember nuances, I find something really wonderful shimmering up at me from the page.

It is these glimmers and sparkles which I latch onto and endeavor to amplify and multiply. I use them as inspiration to help me move through other tough moments as well as to weave a cocoon of light in which I can heal and become stronger.

I have chosen to share my tender moments of reflection as I know the illumination I've found will help brighten others' paths, including yours. By reading my stories, I hope you will learn new ways to find more light in your life...and continue to follow it!

So, with humility, I offer you **Sunflower Wisdom** and send you much love and gratitude for being a part of my journey.

Felicia

Look for the Lessons in Your Journey

I've been in business for myself for over twenty years now. It's hard to believe it's been so long since I dove into the world of self-employment as a massage therapist, spa owner, consultant, mentor, author and speaker. But I can't imagine anything else. I love working for myself, building something out of nothing over and over again. I also love knowing the path I follow in large part is something I build one step at a time as I walk along it.

But...in the journey of entrepreneurship - and in life - there are often detours in the path which appear without warning. Sometimes they take us to places of incredible possibility and prosperity.

Other times they take us into blind alleys, dead-end streets and difficult situations we'd have rather skipped all together. In the former, these unplanned treks into new worlds can totally change us and our businesses in some incredible ways by introducing us to new clients, partners, products, systems or ideas that take us to higher and higher levels. In the latter, the unknown sometimes becomes scary rather than scintillating; hurtful instead of helpful; damaging instead of delightful.

And interestingly enough, what is true for the places of potential possibilities and prosperity can also be true for the dead-ends and difficulties - and vice versa. In fact, no matter which off-road excursions you take, there is the opportunity for good and bad, fear and fearlessness, prosperity and poverty, success and scandal in all of them.

In short, you must be prepared for the best and the worst at every turn. And if you want to succeed despite all the ups and downs, you must be willing to learn from your mistakes or misjudgments and to keep walking the path.

Some people will read this and think, "Oh that's easy for Felicia to say. Look at how successful she is. She has no idea of the problems, challenges, betrayals, etc., that I've had to deal with in my life and business." They'd be both right and wrong.

I'll never know your exact path because I am not you. I have not had your collection of experiences, opportunities, successes, and failures. But I have had mine.

Over the years, through my businesses I have encountered and survived embezzlement, theft, law suits, sexual harassment claims, flooding, bankruptcy and various forms of betrayal by former business associates, clients, friends, staff members and vendors. I have invested - and sometimes lost - tens of thousands of dollars in other people's promises, products or visions. I've experienced guilt by association where people chose not to trust me or my business simply because they'd been burned by **someone else** in the past.

On a personal level, I grew up in a fairly well hidden, but sometimes extreme, level of poverty. Despite having amazing grandparents, I lived through the uncontrolled mental illness of a parent - and all the emotional and physical pain that resulted from it. I dropped out of high school at age sixteen because the level of family problems and drama were such a strain on me, I couldn't cope. Then, before I was twenty years old, I lost my entire immediate family to a collection of terminal illnesses and countless close friends to AIDS.

I could choose to focus on any one of these situations as something to hold me back or keep me from succeeding at a higher level. I could remain angry and hurt about any of these losses or injuries to my heart, wallet or pride. But for my own health and well-being, I instead CHOOSE to see them all as blessings or lessons.

I know that I can ALWAYS find something good or worth learning in any situation...eventually. It may take some time to find it, but I know *there is a gift* waiting for me in every tragedy or trial I encounter if I stop and look for it. This is exactly what **Sunflower Wisdom** - and my earlier book, **The Sunflower Princess: A Healing Fairytale** - are all about.

Whatever challenge you are facing - be it a loss of money, relationship, or reputation through your own mis-steps and misjudgments or those of someone else - look for the lessons and gifts. Is this a situation meant to wake you up so you pay attention? To put you on a new path? To help you to see your own similar faults or mistakes and cause you to make amends?

Was the person who "betrayed" you actually sent to teach you more about yourself? Or how to listen for once and for all to your gut instincts? How to take responsibility for yourself and your actions and choices instead of blaming others for the results you are getting? Or who to put your trust in and when to do so?

I don't know your answers. However, I do know from many past experiences that IF and WHEN you take the time to look past whatever "wrongs" or slights have been committed and whatever "failures" you've had, there is a bigger story and lesson behind them.

I encourage you to look for the lessons and gifts in every problem and crisis - and to be grateful for the opportunity to find them in the midst of a less than perfect situation. When you are able to do this, I believe you will have found true success and the ability to overcome any challenge that comes your way. I hope my book and stories will help you get started on that journey.

Hope is being able to see that there is light despite all of the darkness.

Desmond Tutu

Doing What is Right Vs. Doing What is Right for You

I recently saw this quote from Hafiz: "Stay close to anything that makes you glad you are alive." It made me think about how many things we do in life which don't make us feel great or happy to be doing them.

Have you ever been faced with a personal choice of doing what you "should" do, *ought* to do or what was the "right" thing versus listening to your heart, intuition or even divine guidance and doing what was intended?

Of course, you have. Probably.

To be clear, I'm not talking about smacking that totally obnoxious person at the grocery store upside the head instead of smiling patiently while they loudly talk on their cell phone in the checkout line. Or devouring an entire box of Krispy Kreme's instead of having a lovely, low-fat bran muffin for breakfast.

Those are impulses guided by impatience, frustration, hunger or boredom which would feel satisfying in the moment but could result in serious injury or jail time with the former - and perhaps a need for larger pants with the latter.

No, I am talking about *listening to the call of your heart or soul* to create the life you desire instead of doing what other people think you should do because it fits into the picture of your life THEY have for you.

It's about feeling the pull towards something greater than you ever thought you could do or be and listening to it instead of the opinions of those who said it would be impossible or a failure.

It's doing what is in line with your most authentic self instead of staying with the status quo. And sometimes - unfortunately - it is about disappointing or hurting others by loving yourself more than anyone else or ever before.

True, there are some people who are complete rule followers: those who always think of others first or who - without fail – take the correct action even if it's not what they want or need.

But doing the "right" thing - while considerate, nice and perhaps caring - could also be an act of giving up your spirit or essence one piece at a time instead of deepening your connection to you and the life you were meant to live. Sounds like a slow march to dissatisfaction and resentment to me.

If you are facing a choice between what is "right" versus what is right for you, the advice I can offer is this:

Choose to do, have and be a part of things that make your heart sing, your body tingle and your spirit soar. Allow yourself to FEEL life and get swept away in the wonder and awesomeness of YOU and everything around you. Look for the amazing and incredible whenever possible. Refuse to settle for or focus on the average and status quo.

Be willing to break a few rules to do what is RIGHT for you. As Grace Hopper and many others have said, "It is better to ask for forgiveness than permission." If you wait for everyone else to tell you it is OK to do that which you are destined to do, you may never do it.

TAKE ACTION NOW.

I give you permission…and forgive you ☺

Gratitude Abounds

Back when I was fairly young, very single and working as a waitress at a popular chain restaurant (Darryl's), I used to work on Thanksgiving. We served lunch and dinner all day long on Thanksgiving Day and were swarmed with people who wanted a better-than-cafeteria-style holiday meal without cooking it at home.

Mostly we had older couples, or groups of friends come in, although I'm sure we had a few families as well as single diners. Regardless of who they were, many of the people I waited on were almost apologetic about causing me to have to work that day. However, I was happy to be there, often working a double shift, so other co-workers could travel home or be off with their families.

It may have seemed selfless at the time - and I definitely worked that angle a bit to get better than normal tips. But in all honesty, it was a huge relief for me to be at work all day on Thanksgiving.

Why? Because my own family was dead and gone and I didn't want to be at home alone faced with my intense feelings of grief and abandonment. Even worse, I didn't want to be the "token" charity case who got invited to spend the holiday with someone else's loving family.

Though it would have been nice to be included and enjoy a (hopefully) delicious home-cooked Turkey Day meal, the idea of being a guest/outsider at someone else's familial celebration and witnessing their resulting bliss in being together hurt almost more than being alone. It wouldn't have been MY family.

Sigh.

****

Today, I am so very lucky. I have an incredibly kind, thoughtful and tolerant husband and two funny dogs who envelop me in unconditional love. I also have an extended family with whom I reconnected a few years ago, including seven young cousins who I adore, as well as their parents and grandparents.

Through my husband, I also have in-laws who - though quite quirky - count me as one of their own children as well as a beautiful niece and two nephews. And I have an AMAZING "family" of friends all around the world that encircle me with their loving embraces online and whenever we meet up. I also have days filled with clients and co-workers who I adore, work that inspires me and the deep satisfaction that together we are making a difference in each **other's** lives and the world.

At times our own light goes out and is rekindled by a spark from another person. Each of us has cause to think with deep gratitude of those who have lighted the flame within us.

Albert Schweitzer

So, despite the empty spots which remain in my life where my parents and grandparents used to be, my life and heart are full to the point of overflowing. Perhaps these spaces had to be created for me to fill them with even more love, gratitude and compassion than I knew were possible.

I am grateful for my overflowing cup and to everyone in my life for all they have brought to it past, present and future.

Finding Inspiration in Water

One of my favorite travel rituals is to go for a run in a local park or other scenic/historic area. It doesn't get much more scenic than in Niagara Falls - and the weather was perfect one fall day when I was in the area to teach at the Canadian Massage Conference.

No matter where I go, teaching at conferences - particularly in the Massage Industry - and in places like Niagara Falls is such a blessing in several ways:

1) I have some space and time away from my usual day to day routine/craziness to clear my head and be able to think.

2) I get to be with some of my favorite people in the world. They inspire me and surround me with love, light and lots of hugs.

3) I get to teach, inspire and learn from my students.

4) The natural beauty I encounter can be renewing, relaxing and simply awe inspiring.

As I was running beside the falls on this trip, I had a chance to think about how amazing water is and what a metaphor it is for life, our journeys, and even people. Some things I pondered...

- Water can be calm, beautiful, soothing, soft, deep, refreshing and silent. It can cascade, trickle, pool and come in ripples or waves.

- It can also be raging, rushing, angry, hard, shallow, rough and roaring. It can show up pouring, in torrents, floods, and rapids.

- When it comes up against obstacles, water goes around or over them - sometimes even right through them. It doesn't ask questions or hesitate when it has a destination in mind.

- Water is determined and persistent to the point of sometimes eroding the foundation or the actual path it was trying to travel, creating a new path in the process. But it does what it wants and is created to do. Period.

- Water is incredibly empathic. It takes on new forms because of the conditions of the elements around it. When the air is cool, water can become fog or ice - when it's hot it can become steam or simply hot water. If the sky is cloudy, water reflects that back just as it brings even more light to sun-shiny days.

Like water, I can be and do many of these things, but I can do something water can't. I can DECIDE to be different than the circumstances or moods around me. I can CHOOSE to go around or simply ignore obstacles I encounter as well as decide that maybe it's a better option to choose a new path.

I can keep my cool in a heated argument instead of allowing my temper to boil over; stay calm and un-rippled despite a rough or windy day; intend to bring warmth and comfort to those I touch even though they may be trying to turn me to ice.

I can't be by Niagara Falls all the time, but I will continue to allow its' beauty and power to inspire me to be like water in a few key ways: to go with the flow; to gracefully ride the waves and tides that come; and to do my best to be a source of inspiration, peace and renewal to all that come to my shore.

How Louise Hay Keeps Helping Me

I first read one of Louise Hay's books when I was a new massage therapist in the mid-1990s. At the time, I was really beginning to delve into my own healing and found her story and words to be very helpful and inspiring.

Every once in a while, I pick up one of her books again and remind myself of some simple ways to take care of myself, heal from new and old wounds and move on with my life. One book I use again and again is *You Can Heal Your Life**.

Though a number of ideas and exercises ring true for again and again, there is one technique I have put into practice almost every day, especially when I am struggling with something that is challenging or painful. It is simply stating some positive affirmations about letting go. I truly believe by letting go of what is not working or what is no longer needed in our lives, we make space for what we really want to have, be and attract.

So. if you ever see me driving down the road talking to myself, here are a few things I might be saying:

I am willing to let go. I release. I let go.
I release all stress and tension.
I release all pain and restriction.
I release all fear and anxiety.
I release all sadness and grief.
I release all anger and resentment
I release all guilt and sorrow.
I let go of everything that no longer serves me.
I let go of all old limitations.

*There is a list of all books, articles and resources mentioned at the back of the book. It includes links and websites as appropriate. ☺

I let go and I am at peace.
I am at peace with the process of life.
I am at peace with the past.
I am at peace with the present.
I am at peace with myself.
I am at peace.
I am safe.

To attract something positive into the space left I usually add:

"I am open to receive all the abundance and happiness the Universe has for me. I easily attract and accept all the prosperity, love, joy and positive energy that is available for me."

These affirmations may not be the perfect fit for you, but they have worked well for me. Whatever type of affirmation you choose, remember to use words and phrases that bring you peace, power, energy and positive thoughts about yourself as well as what you want in your life, relationships, career or business.

Every thought we think is creating our future.

Louise L. Hay

Perseverance – A Lifelong Lesson

We've all got issues and problems to deal with in our time on this earth. Whether you face struggles in your business or personal life, some days things seem too much to bear.

Probably the lesson I remember most from my childhood and that has been the most valuable to me in terms of getting through the ups and downs of life and business has been the lesson of perseverance. From the time I was really young, my grandparents told me story after story about not giving up. Both had lived through the depression as well as many of their own health problems and were still around to tell me about it well into in their eighties and nineties.

Some examples which come to mind about their "stick-to-it-ive-ness" – a term I heard from them a lot:

- My grandfather worked for seven years to be able to save the money up for *one semester* of college. He obviously proved himself as he earned a full academic scholarship and ended up getting his PhD in education. He later became a much loved and well-respected college professor and dean at numerous colleges, including NYU.

- My grandfather also survived a number of nearly fatal illnesses including a ruptured appendix as a teen and massive heart attack later in life. He also survived a diagnosis of terminal prostate cancer by more than ten years past the original (and thankfully inaccurate) prognosis… as well as the doctor who gave it to him.

- My grandmother told me many tales about her crazy travel adventures through Alabama and the Midwest. They often involved just missing natural disasters like tornadoes while somehow still making it to her destination...eventually but safely.

- My grandmother was also an ordained Methodist minister – something that was practically unheard of back in the early 1900's. No doubt the dedicated pursuit of her education and achievement of what she wanted required a lot of perseverance.

When I was about seven or eight, my grandparents gave me a copy of a book I will never forget called *Never Quit* by Glenn Cunningham. (You can also read about him in *American Miler: The Life & Times of Glenn Cunningham* by Paul Keill.) Glenn, who set the record for the mile in the 1930s, had met my grandfather at some point when he was teaching in New York.

As a child, Glenn had been burned severely by a woodstove explosion that killed his brother. Doctor's had nearly amputated his legs and told his parent's he'd never walk again. But as Glenn struggled to recover through unimaginable pain, he heard over and over in his mind his own father's words, "A Cunningham never quits."

Somehow through all his challenges, Glenn was not only able to defy the odds and diagnosis and walk again, but he also became one of the most well-known track runners of the 1930s and was on the 1932 & 1936 US Olympic Teams.

To this day, that book sits on my book shelf along with many others which urge me to keep going when times are tough and keep working toward the things I really want in life. I've read it several times and am always inspired by it!

No matter what is going on in your life, whether your business is struggling, you've been laid off, gotten a divorce or are fighting to overcome other personal or health challenges, know that you can make it through. You have what it takes inside yourself to keep going, to find a better way or to accept the hand that has been dealt you and make the best of it.

I say all this because I know it's true. Over my life I've found again and again, the difficulties I've encountered have been some of the best teachers I've ever had AND have reminded me of what really matters to me in life. Time and time again, they've also reawakened my passion and talent for perseverance. I know I can do what it takes to get where I want to be - and so can you.

I am forever grateful for the many stories and examples of perseverance my loving grandparents shared with me. I continue to pass on their wisdom by writing and speaking about my own experiences of persistence whenever possible. I hope you will too.

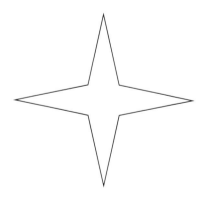

Adversity has the effect of eliciting talents, which in prosperous circumstances would have lain dormant.

Horace

Looking for Signals

Is it possible that committing suicide was my mother's destiny? That it served a higher purpose for her life or mine? That it was intended to teach me about myself or life in a way that nothing else could? Could it have been done as a loving gesture of some type or even an act of kindness?

I have not really pondered these sorts of questions before although I am a big believer in the idea that everything happens for a reason, no matter what it is or how it is perceived through human eyes as "good" or "bad."

I just read, *Signals: An Inspiring Story of Life After Life* by Joel Rothschild which metaphorically fell off the bookshelf into my hands. In the book, Joel talks about his dearest friend Albert who committed suicide. Albert was gay, living with AIDS and evidently had an incredibly tender heart and tortured soul. The description of his difficulties in life while not the same as those my mother faced, mirrored her experience or at least my impression of it in a number of ways.

Like Albert, my mother, Beth, befriended a number of people who were abandoned or helpless or unwanted in some kind of way. She seemed to provide a friendship-based half-way house for gay men who need the acceptance of an older female figure.

Beth gave these dear souls a place where they could be themselves without fear or judgment about who they were with or what they did in their lives or bedrooms. Unfortunately, the kind spirit which allowed my mom to be non-judgmental also left her with a lack of judgment which did not always serve her well.

Often it seemed she got the raw end of the deal, especially later in her life when opportunistic people would take advantage of her open, giving and sometimes naïve nature.

Also similar to Albert, my mother had a very tender heart which was broken over and over again by people and the world. As I was growing up, she repeatedly told me stories of small insults and injuries to her heart by mean-spirited people who had treated her poorly.

Looking for love in all the wrong places I guess or perhaps just leaving herself open to the pain that people would unwittingly or unknowingly cause by disappointing her. She was victimized in one way or another by people she trusted throughout her life. This made me sad for her. At the same time, I was confused as to how these things happened so often, as if she never learned her lesson. Perhaps it was just not something she was capable of doing.

When I read about Albert's suicide, line after line resonated within me. Joel, the author, talked about how by committing suicide, Albert had broken every promise he'd ever made to him. That is how I felt when Beth died, at least in part. I felt she had completely reneged on her agreement to be my mother and to love me.

In retrospect, I realize Beth never promised me much. In fact, I can't really remember any declarations from her other telling me she loved me and that I could do whatever I wanted as long as I didn't hurt anyone else.

I guess what I thought she meant by that comment was that she wouldn't ever hurt me, but God, we know that isn't true. She hurt and disappointed me by not being there; by not calling or coming over when she said she might; by not inviting me to stay over at her house; by not being "normal" around my friends.

And then were the times when she physically hurt me or wounded me with her threats of no financial support; no help in taking care of "my" house; all her attacks and spells and craziness and pain and sickness and depression…all of it…she hurt me over and over and over again.

Perhaps her suicide was her way of attempting to put an end to my pain along with hers, although that is not exactly how it worked out. Still eighteen years later I am struggling to figure out what it all meant, why it happened and how she could do that to me.

*****

One of my most vivid memories – actually it is a story which was told to me, not something I went through or remember – is that of my mother's near-death experience (NDE).

When I was three and she was thirty-four, my mother had a massive heart attack and died. She was brought back to life somehow and obviously recovered to live another seventeen years. But in all the times she talked about her NDE, she always referred to it with such wistfulness and told me repeatedly how she really didn't want to come back.

Beth described where she went during that time as being lush and green with rolling pastures under a perfect sky, what she thought Ireland looked like. She remembered it as being truly serene and beautiful, and a place where she was completely happy.

From the way she explained it, I have to believe she had never felt that way …happy that is… before or after. Since reading Joel's book, I have begun to wonder if perhaps by coming back from that near-death experience, her inner turmoil increased somewhat.

That rather than feeling like every day of life was an incredible gift not to be taken for granted, it seemed she looked at it as a penance or punishment she had to endure. That she was just passing her time and trying to make it through one day after another until she could finally get back to the place where she really wanted to be. That having seen what she felt was heaven, she now looked at every day here as even more torturous and unbearable. "Hell on earth," I remember her saying.

So where is Beth now and what is she feeling? Is the place she's gone to everything she thought it would be? Free of pain, sorrow, suffering and Junior League socials? Is she at some giant disco in the sky sitting on top of a speaker hanging out with all her favorite buddies who died from AIDS?

Or is she in a garden up to her elbows in potting soil and daylilies, with a bag of knitting or embroidery close by? Is my grandmother there with her working on her painting and my grandfather doing some of the puzzles he liked to do, or perhaps fly fishing? And what about my dad? Is he driving them all crazy with his idiosyncrasies? Are they all fighting about who will get to visit me in my dreams next?

Is Beth saying it's her turn because she knows I am still upset and now wondering if or why I should consider being a mother? Does she know I am questioning it because I am afraid I'm too much like her and could hurt a child the way she hurt me?

Or is it because Beth is the one who left in such a violent and (perceived) selfish way? That she left me by choice when no one else had a choice in the matter? That she left when we were finally starting to repair our broken relationship a little?

Or is that why she stays away? Because she knows her actions still hurt me? Because she knows that I am not ready to see her? Is that why she sends my grandmother to take care of me in my dreams, just like she did in life. Does she know my mother-bond is really with Pearle, who loves me best and will do the better job?

Pearle is the one who knows the right songs to sing to put me to sleep. She knows how to rub my back in just the right way and how to make me warm milk toast when my tummy feels bad. She knows all my favorite things and gives the best hugs and takes me for ice cream as a special treat.

When Pearle says my name, it is like a beautiful symphony I want to hear more of. When my mother says it, I hesitate out of the fear and unknowing of whether it is a good day or a bad day. My name from Beth's lips causes me to tiptoe around the house, avoiding her potential bad mood and being roped into her web of guilt for one thing or another.

I don't want to be like her. Don't want to be sick or in pain or depressed or just plain depressing. I want to be fun and free and for people to love and respect me. I want to give them things to be proud of and to be dependable. To be someone they can count on and lean on in good times and bad.

And I want to get better with each passing day and year, more interesting, more intelligent, more loving and lovable. I want to complain less and be a better person. I want to make more money and give more away. I want to inspire people to be their best by setting the example of doing the same.

*Every moment of light
and dark is a miracle.*

Walt Whitman

Life Goes On

I recently saw this article, _Farewell to my daughter Kate, who died on Christmas Day,_ by Jean Gross. It was posted on Facebook by my friend Angie, still grieving for her older brother who died unexpectedly on June 17th a few years ago. Angie is incredibly loving, thoughtful, and deep. Since she shared it, I knew the article would be worth reading. I wasn't disappointed.

The column talks about the untimely death of the Jean's thirty-six - year-old daughter. I say "untimely" not just because she passed on Christmas Day, but also because she left behind a young family with two small children...children who were _anxiously_ waiting to open their Christmas presents despite the somber event which had just occurred. Talk about bad timing.

They say death does not wait, but then sometimes neither does life. So poor Jean had to juggle conversations with Hospice and the undertaker while cooking a turkey and watching her grandkids unwrap their stockings. Wow.

Though some people may not be able to identify with all the "must-do" holiday tasks and responsibilities the grieving mother and grandmother faced just moments after her daughter slipped away, I do and had a similar experience.

More than thirty years ago, after four years of teetering on the edge of life and death after suffering a massive stroke, my beloved grandmother was finally ready to let go. Just four days earlier on June 13th and what would have been my grandparents' 49th wedding anniversary, I'd had "the talk" with my grandmother. As I laid in bed snuggled up beside her that evening, I told Pearle through choked back tears I would be OK without her.

Thinking about it now, I am still overcome by emotion for the sheer courage and maturity it took a sixteen-year-old girl to initiate that conversation.

I don't remember if she rubbed my back or I rubbed hers, probably both, but we hugged each other close and did our best to console each other in this tenderly awful moment. I never wanted to see her leave or tell her she could go. But I also knew it was time to stop being selfish and finally give her the permission she'd waited far too long to receive.

After that night, my grandmother's condition deteriorated rapidly and by the next day, she was no longer able to speak. I knew I'd done the right thing by having the talk the night before and could see at least her body was trying to comply. Yet, still she held on.

On the morning of June 17th, it was clear the end was coming. My mother and I took turns sitting with my grandmother and waiting for the inevitable. Unexpectedly, during one of my sessions with her, the doorbell rang so I walked away to answer it. Two older women from our church had stopped by to pay a visit to their dear friend. I let them in and excused myself to see if she was "decent" enough for them to look in on her and say hello. But in the brief moment while I was away at the door, my grandmother decided it was time to leave. She was gone.

I'm not sure how to explain the flurry of what happened next, but it was unlike anything I'd ever experienced before. As soon as I realized she was dead, I ran to the bathroom and threw up. Then, I had to tell the two visitors they were simply too late. One of the ladies nearly fainted and had to sit down and fan herself to regain composure. The other was clearly torn between comforting me and staying by her friend, unfortunately adding more to my stress.

Meanwhile, as soon as I told her the news, my mother - a woman well-known for her high levels of drama during even the best of times - began wailing at the top of her lungs. She ignored everyone else and immediately barricaded herself in her bedroom, but not before turning on the stereo and blasting a meaningful yet blaringly loud version of Beethoven's *Moonlight Sonata* through the entire house.

There I was – a teenager - dealing with a crazy woman, two unexpected visitors, one on the border of hysteria, and a dead body – while my eardrums threaten to bleed from classical piano. None of the adults in the house were of any help to me, so I did the only thing I could think to do. I called the cemetery where my father and grandfather were buried for advice.

I can only imagine the shock the receptionist there got when I called. The conversation went something like this:

"Thank you for calling Westminster Gardens. How can I help you?"

"Hi. I, um, have a problem. My grandfather and father are buried there and, um, my grandmother just died and I'm not sure what to do. I was wondering if you could help me?"

"Of course, honey. Do you know when the funeral is going to be?"

"Well, I mean my grandmother *just* died, like ten minutes ago, and I'm not sure who to call or what I am supposed to do about...um…her body."

Awkward pause...

"Oh....I see. Well. Do you have a minister you can call?"

"Yes."

"OK good. You should probably start by calling him. Do you know the funeral home you're going to use?"

"No, I'm not sure. I guess my mom knows."

"Oh good, your mom. Isn't she there to help you?"

"Well she is here, but right now she's locked herself in her bedroom. I don't think she can help me."

"Oh, I see. Well, why don't you call the minister first and see if he knows about your grandmother's final arrangements."

"OK. I guess I'll do that."

"If you need anything else you just call us back, OK?"

"OK, thank you."

I hung up the phone, made a couple more calls, and went back to figure out what to do with my guests. To be honest, I felt oddly terrible about how their visit turned out. That emotion faded quickly, however, as I was suddenly even more horrified to realize that very soon *other people* – perhaps a lot of them - would be showing up or stopping by to bring by food or "comfort" my family.

In that moment, *all I could think about* was what a mess our house was and immediately started cleaning up. Before the visiting women could get out the door, I was sweeping our living room floor, practically pushing the broom under their feet. After they left, I turned into a little whirlwind, trying to make our house more presentable before the men from the funeral home or the minster got there.

My boyfriend arrived just as the people from the funeral home were driving away and got upset with me that I didn't keep "Grandma" around until he could say goodbye. I remember thinking how incredibly wrong his reaction seemed - especially when I had SO much more to do than worry about how he felt about MY grandmother dying. What nerve! But the anger and grief combination fueled my cleaning frenzy and I got pretty much everything in order.

*****

The days after my grandmother's death are mostly a blur. I believe I was so focused keeping everything and everyone around me (mainly my mom) moving forward that I don't think I even cried until her memorial service. My reaction may seem odd to some, but the truth is you never truly know exactly how you will respond to situation until you're in it. At least I didn't have to make a turkey!

Eventually, though, the dam broke. I've never missed someone so much in all my life as I missed my grandmother then - and even almost thirty years later - as I miss her now. At times, the ache and emptiness inside my heart has been almost paralyzing. There were days in those early years when I didn't know how to go on, or even if I could face the world without her.

But like death, life doesn't wait. Whether you have company coming over or you just have to go back to work again, life instead must go on. Sometimes it seems like nothing you do makes a difference in your world or anyone else's.

You're trying to make it through each day the best you can, but the searing pain is still there, jabbing you in the heart and knocking the wind out of you around every corner until you feel like you can't move.

Still, the house has to get cleaned, dinner has to get made and eventually, Christmas presents will have to be bought and opened again. Life has to move on - *and it is OK that it does.*

As I look back this picture of Pearle from around 1980, I see so much of her in me and realize that in a big way, my grandmother never really left. She and I are a lot a like - we're both Sagittarians, teachers, writers and problem solvers.

Like my grandmother, I am often up until the wee hours of the night, typing away on whatever I'm writing at the moment, sitting *at the very same desk* she did in the picture above, surrounded by mounds of books and tons of projects that need to be completed. Through the impact she made on who I am and all I do, she is still here. *And through me, in some sense, her life goes on too.*

If you are going through a loss, know that you are not alone. Whoever you've lost is still with you in your heart and memories, maybe even in your furniture:-). They'll totally understand it when *your life* has to go on.

Life Goes On – Again

In the last couple of weeks, a couple of my former, regular massage clients have passed away as well as a past co-worker. They were 78, 62 and 48. One death was seemingly expected - that of the oldest. The others appear to have been a complete and total shock to those around them.

I had not seen any of these folks in at least five years, much longer in two cases. So, in terms of impact in my life, day-to-day, really nothing is different. I won't miss them from my schedule nor notice their absence at a party I'm attending. But each of their losses still creates a unique hole in my heart which can never be filled.

As I've shared, I experienced a lot of loss in my early life, so in a way, I am not ever surprised by these kinds of things. Death is a part of life that can creep up when you least expect it. However, it seems as I get older, what makes me saddest about people dying is the idea that certain chapters or parts of my life are over for good. That there will never be a reunion where Jim and I will joke about old times at the Ice Chalet, nor will I have the chance to put the minds and bodies of my former clients into a state of relaxed bliss.

So where is the silver lining in death, especially the unexpected death? I guess quite simply it is that life does go on despite the loss of these people - or any of us for that matter. Grass will still grow, rain will still fall, and the seasons will continue to change.

It is hard for the families and friends who are hurting from loss right now to see this. At first, they will be suspended in their sorrow and grief, wishing time would go backward to a day when their loved one was still alive. Instead they are faced to move forward into a future where those who have passed will never be.

But eventually, like sunflowers, they too will be able find the light; to lift their heads and begin to see their lives are still there, waiting for them. When they do, they will likely have a renewed sense of wanting to live more fully, to be present and to cherish those they love and care about. This, to me, is often the biggest gift for those left behind after a death and one I do my best to remember.

Death is not extinguishing the light;
it is only putting out the lamp
because the dawn has come.

Rabindranath Tagore

Many Friends, Many Visits

I experienced a lot of loss in my life at an early age. Between the time I was ten and twenty, I lost my mother, father and my beloved maternal grandparents, who were actually raising me. In the same period as well as afterwards, many of my mother's closest friends – several of whom were like older brothers or father figures to me - died from AIDS. At times, the grief was crushing.

Many of those who died have come to me in my dreams after they passed. The first were my father and grandfather who died two years apart. Both would appear in my dreams – separately, not together - to let me know they loved me and that they were ok. After Pearle died several years later, she followed suit and often came to "check-in" on me while I slept.

Three of my mother's friends who died also visited me in my dreams. Two of them - who could never bring themselves to tell anyone they were sick - came to tell me they were sorry for concealing their illness and explain why they did.

But my mother was a different story. Unlike the other family members and friends who died, her death was quite sudden. Both of my grandparents and my father had suffered from terminal illnesses that played out over months or years, giving us plenty of time to tie up loose ends and say our goodbyes.

Beth, who suffered for years with manic depression and perhaps other forms of mental illness, committed suicide unexpectedly when I was twenty.

Although she tried to take her life at least once before when I was in high school, there had been no obvious warning signs or comments to cause me to think she would end it all when she did. In fact, my last conversation with my mother was a pretty heated argument – one in which I told essentially her she needed to take responsibility for her own life and happiness. In a way, I guess she did in that by ending her life.

At any rate, after she died, I didn't have any healing dreams or visits from her like I had with other family members. Instead there were only upsetting nightmares which caused me more grief and anger towards her than I already felt.

Several years passed and I worked to put her death out of my mind. Initially, I moved back to Colorado in an attempt to work things out with my boyfriend out there but came back to North Carolina after a year and a half. Soon after he and I broke up. I had a few other unsuccessful relationships and eventually decided to seek counseling to help improve my romantic relations.

Though the counselor and I talked about a variety of things, one day, the session unexpectedly turned onto the topic of my mother. Quickly, it became abundantly clear through my buckets of tears that my anger and resentment about her suicide were definitely not gone.

We ran out of time before I could get all my thoughts out, so the counselor sent me home tasked with writing a letter to my mother. Basically, she wanted me to express my feelings about what my mom had done. I don't remember what I put in the letter exactly, but know there were questions of "Why did you do it?" and "How could you abandon me?" The rest is just an emotional, teary blur.

What I do recall specifically is exactly how I ended the letter: "Can you even hear me? Let me know!"

By the next day though, I had completely forgotten about the appointment with the counselor and my writing assignment. I did my homework for school and then rushed off to work at my restaurant job. At the end of the shift, I went into the bathroom to change clothes before relaxing and having a drink at the bar with my new boyfriend and co-workers.

As I was getting dressed, I heard with unmistakable clarity Beethoven's Moonlight Sonata playing. The restaurant was in an old building and had no speakers in the bathroom or anywhere nearby, yet I heard the music as though it was right in the room with me. I scrambled into my clothes and ran out to the bar to see if it could be on the television out there. It wasn't, nor was it playing on either of the two music systems we had in the restaurant.

Had it been any other song, even any other piano concerto, I wouldn't have thought much about it. But in our family, Moonlight Sonata is very significant. When I was little, my grandmother would play it on the piano for me almost every night at bedtime, as would my mother if I was with her. In fact, my mother – a classically trained pianist - had made an audio tape of herself playing Moonlight Sonata, which we played at my grandmother's memorial service as well as my mother's.

I knew without question the phantom piano music was somehow sent from my mother. Though she didn't answer of my other questions, Beth was letting me know she heard me. I wish I could say I felt comforted by that visitation, but to be honest it scared the crap out of me.

The relationship my mom and I had was a bit rocky, especially during the last few years of her life. Even though we'd been working to repair it and had been on relatively good terms when she died, I was afraid of her. Her visitation brought up a fear in me that she was coming back to haunt me from the afterlife just the way she had "haunted" me when she was living. It didn't go away nor did my grief and anger.

It was probably about seven years later when my mother paid me another visit. My newest boyfriend and I had just watched the movie, "The Sixth Sense." With so many losses and "visits" I'm a firm believer people can communicate from the other side, and the movie left me feeling quite emotional.

That night, I dreamt I was lying on the couch in my living room. A bright white light with no particular shape or features hovered above me and I was paralyzed, unable to move, speak or even fully open my eyes. The light did not talk to me, but still I knew it was my mother. And for the first time since she died, I felt she was there only to convey love.

I woke up with a sense of peace about my mother I had not felt, possibly ever. I think she was finally starting to move past her own heartache and pain to heal and experience love again. It was nice to feel it.

Many years have passed since then, and I still struggle to heal the pain of losing my mother. However, after having that dream, I was able to begin making tangible steps to move beyond the loss and focus on the love. I hope she has too.

Why I Didn't Say Hello

The other day, I saw an old friend - literally just SAW her - across a crowded bar. After a long day at work, I was on my way in to drop off a gift for another friend — a talented vocalist - who was performing that night. I was exhausted, hadn't had dinner, and had no plans of staying any longer than it took to drop off the present.

But when I saw my old friend, I paused for a brief moment and wondered if I should stop and say hello.

I didn't - and here's why.

Several years ago, we had a falling out - a bad one - and one that was mostly my fault. It was a business issue but one which felt very personal to her I'm sure. Though my intentions were good, they came across otherwise and caused our friendship to end.

I felt terrible about it then and still hate that I caused her any pain. Initially, I apologized several times and have reached out a number of times in small ways. Yet we have not spoken directly or seen each other in person in years. Thus, I knew that a simple "hello" would most likely not be possible.

At a minimum, I would have been totally ignored or snubbed. At worst, I might have reopened a painful wound - or even anger - in her that's been simmering since we last met, causing an unexpected confrontation. Most likely, it would have been something in between - a stiff exchange of pleasantries at best — which would have left us both feeling unsettled.

Perhaps it seems like a cowardly thing to do, but my choice was to do nothing. I walked past as though I had not seen her, dropped off my gift, and left the bar as I had originally planned.

One of the BEST pieces of advice I ever got about dealing with conflict basically says if you aren't sure whether your words or actions will make a situation better - or at least not worse - then it is better to do nothing. I have used this wisdom and advice many times when my temper and impulses may have pushed me in another direction. I can say with almost 100% certainty that doing nothing is often the wisest choice I can make. On this day at least, facing the potential conflict was not a good option for me.

Then, a day or two later, I saw this quote from José Micard Teixeira (not Meryl Streep, as some people attribute it). It fits in with my choice as well, because I recognize to some extent, I do get to CHOOSE the situations I put myself in.

I no longer have patience for certain things, not because I've become arrogant, but simply because I reached a point in my life where I do not want to waste more time with what displeases me or hurts me. I have no patience for cynicism, excessive criticism and demands of any nature. I lost the will to please those who do not like me, to love those who do not love me and to smile at those who do not want to smile at me.

I no longer spend a single minute on those who lie or want to manipulate. I decided not to coexist anymore with pretense, hypocrisy, dishonesty and cheap praise. I do not tolerate selective erudition nor academic arrogance. I do not adjust either to popular gossiping.

I hate conflict and comparisons. I believe in a world of opposites and that's why I avoid people with rigid and inflexible personalities. In friendship I dislike the lack of loyalty and betrayal. I do not get along with those who do not know how to give a compliment or a word of encouragement.

Exaggerations bore me, and I have difficulty accepting those who do not like animals. And on top of everything I have no patience for anyone who does not deserve my patience.

It's highly unlikely she is reading this, but just in case…

J, please know I am truly sorry for what happened and for causing you any pain. I hope someday you will forgive me. I know we are both exactly where we are supposed to be in our lives despite our falling out - or perhaps because of it. I wish you well in all you do and thank you for your past friendship and support. Namaste.

Doing nothing IS doing something, at least in situations like this. I'd so thankful I learned this all those years ago. I have no doubt it's saved me from a lot of "somethings" I want nothing to do with!

A fool is known by his speech; and a wise man by his silence.

Pythagoras

Good judgement comes from experience, and a lot of that comes from bad judgement.

Will Rogers

Is Failure Really a Bad Thing?

I always tell people if you aren't failing, you aren't trying. That is to say, in order to succeed you will have failures along the way. In various sales trainings I've attended over the years, I've also heard the idea that every "no" takes you closer to a "yes."

Looking back on various "failures" I've experienced in my life both personally and professionally, I now know that a) they helped make me and my life what they are and b) I probably wouldn't have wanted many of those ventures or relationships to "succeed" in the long-term anyway. In fact, failure is an amazing teacher and one that is often more effective than any class you could enroll in - well as long as you do learn from it!

I've always believed knowledge which isn't shared is to some degree wasted and have long endeavoured to share my own experiences - good and bad - for the betterment of others. As such, I've written about my own failures and struggles in blogs, books and articles including one on how I dealt with the after-math of closing a spa a few years ago. That was a tough piece to write!

Two of my books share my perspective on some of my past "failed" relationships in a fairly revealing and personal way. The first one, **The Sunflower Princess: A Healing Fairy Tale** is a story I wrote many years ago. Though it was originally a love story, it actually became more of a memoir about my life prior to that time - and one which was really quite lonely despite a constant stream of romantic relationships and plenty of friends. Told as a fairy tale, it describes the evolution of my feelings during a period of deep grief and loneliness and shares a number of messages of hope for the reader.

The other, **Reflections of my Heart: A Poetic Journey of Love, Life, Heartbreak and Healing**, is a collection of poetry written about my struggles around personal and romantic relationships. In a sense it is a "pre-quel" to **The Sunflower Princess** and gives the reader an idea of the depth of my pain, loneliness and longing. (Note: I do not take after Taylor Swift. Thus none of the men I dated are easily identifiable or named other than my husband and a very dear friend who was killed in the mid-1990s).

Admittedly, it is somewhat humbling for me to share these "failures" and difficulties in my life with others, especially the romantic ones. But I really feel others will benefit from knowing they are not the only ones out there going through some tough stuff. The goal in publishing these books – including this one - is to provide hope and healing for others dealing with their own situations of grief, loneliness and struggle - and to show there is life on the other side of every loss, past relationship and difficulty. To that end, I will continue to bare my soul and share my stories as well as the learning or questioning which comes from my journey.

My hope is to set an example other people can model. I want others to know that, no matter what you are going through, if you try your best to handle tough situations with grace and love, or at least learn from them, you will inspire others. People are watching those around them, looking for beacons of hope. Perhaps you will be one who gives someone else the courage to keep on trying.

Giving Back & Getting Through

Today is my birthday. Several years ago, on this same day, I read a deeply touching column in our local paper's weekly entertainment/living section. In it, the author, Addison Ore, was writing about her difficulty with celebrating the holidays due to her intense struggle with grief after the loss of her parents and another significant relationship. Below is the email response I sent to her. I share it here as I think it may be helpful for anyone who has difficulty dealing with the holidays due to loss, grief or depression.

It may seem weird to share this. However, at the moment the winter holidays are in full swing. With my birthday smashed right in the middle of all the various celebrations, this day and time of year can be a struggle for me too. Like many of you, I feel better when I can do things to help others - even on my birthday - and I hope my "gift" to Addison will also help you.

Though I've been without my parents - and the grandparents who actually raised me - for a bit longer than you have, I so sympathize and appreciate your need to let go of the past. For years the holidays for me have been more bitter than sweet and the few traditions that I shared with my family during my childhood and teen years can cause me sadness still - even though it's been 20+ years since they've all passed on.

I have added some of my own traditions with my husband and his family, but most importantly I make the effort do kind and nurturing things for myself at this time of year. As my birthday falls between Thanksgiving and Christmas (it's today actually), I am lucky that I also get some extra attention and love from the people in my life right about now.

But the most uplifting things are often things I do for myself.

Top of the list - getting massages and spa services. Go figure, since I am a massage therapist and spa owner. But I also take myself out for solo lunches and dinners when I need to treat myself but don't feel like the pressure of company.

I read books I love, write, take baths, do a little shopping, exercise, snuggle up a little more often with my dogs - just anything that gives me a boost.

I try to find a way to do something for other people who have a struggle of some kind, like donating gifts for the patrons of Meals on Wheels, which makes me feel grateful for all that I do have. And I'm not afraid of utilizing an occasional anti-anxiety medication if I have to:-)

(Note - in recent years I've also started putting reindeer antlers - and a red nose - on my car and occasionally try to get my pets into the holiday spirit with cute hats - which does not last long.)

But when I feel those familiar holiday blues peeking around the corner despite my best efforts, I allow myself to feel them, take a nap, or skip that holiday event that just seems like too much. This isn't always popular with people who don't understand why I "don't like Christmas" or can't stand listening to non-stop Christmas music from November 15th to December 31st.

But I truly believe it's more important to honor yourself, especially in times with such emotional ties and memories, than to fake your way through another chorus of "Jingle Bells" for the sake of someone else's holiday spirit or tradition.

*Whatever "traditions of caring" you decide to start for yourself, just know that **you are not alone in your aloneness**. My deepest sympathies for your losses, along with best wishes for the holidays and your continued healing.*

****

And now, true to form, I'm off to have a day of relaxation and things I enjoy for my birthday - working out + sauna and hot tub at gym, pedicure, lunch with a friend, massage, movie and dinner with husband. I think some shopping may happen in there somewhere as well! Happy Birthday to me:-)

During the holiday season - and any time you are trying to heal yourself - schedule some YOU time whether that is to take a nap, read a book, get a massage or cuddle up with your pets. There's no need to force yourself to "celebrate" any holiday or occasion the way other thing you must or should, especially when you are hurting. Be good to yourself and snuggle into loving yourself a little deeper.

I will love the light for it shows me the way, yet I will endure the darkness because it shows me the stars.

Og Mandino

My Beautiful, Ugly, Glittery, Rash of Grief

I just read an awesome article on NewYorkTimes.com - _Getting Grief Right_ - about what grief is really like. In it, Patrick O'Malley talks about his client who "remained in deep despair" and "...was exhausted from acting better than she felt around co-workers, friends and family" long after what she - and probably others - felt was an acceptable time to grieve. She wondered what was wrong with her and did her best to put up a false front for everyone else's sale.

The truth is, grief is one of those things that has a mind of its own and will leave when it is damn well good and ready. Then when you think it's gone for good, it will leap up from beneath the creaking floorboards and drag you down into a deeper, darker place than you'd been before.

Yet, grief is not always a bad thing.

In fact, one of the defining factors in my life - and my development into the person I am now - is the deep grief that started when I was only 10 years old and my father died from lung cancer. I remember getting out of school for a week or so "to mourn" and then going back to a classroom of friends who looked at me as if I had glittery, purple spots all over my face and body - at once both scary and compelling.

In some ways my classmates were intrigued by this new look and "difference" between me and them. Some wanted to ambush me with questions and observations about this thing they'd never seen or heard of before. Others seemed to be afraid the weird, purple rash I'd brought back to school was what had killed my father - and that if they got too close - their fathers might die too.

So, most of my fellow fourth-graders kept their distance until the obvious appearance of the spots and my grief grew weaker and only invisible yet painful scars remained on the inside of my heart and soul. I did my best to hide all traces of it and make them forget there was anything different about me. Even then, I think a few could not forget my "rash" and never got as close to me as they once had been.

As the next few years went by, my grief grew bigger and deeper as I also lost my maternal grandparents with whom I lived*. The worst loss was that of my grandmother, Pearle. She was really my mother in all senses of the word other than actually giving birth to me and probably who I miss the most. I wrote more about her in the story *Life Goes On* a few pages back in this book.

Then, when I was twenty, my mom took her own life and left me to be an adult orphan. This loss was different and instead of just the deep sense of sorrow I'd felt with the others, it came with intense anger at her for abandoning me when I was already so alone. My ugly purple spots returned with a vengeance, becoming swollen and incredibly sensitive to the slightest provocation.

Like the client in the NY Times article, I too put forth a persona of strength which I wore when out in the world. However, at home in private times, mostly on Sundays when I took a rare break from my workaholic tendencies, the pain from these deep wounds would roar up like a demon and paralyze me over and over. It's been over thirty-five years after that first taste of loss and grief, yet it still happens from time to time.

Time passes, and we must move on from our losses. We must also honor the fact that like life, the pain of loss also goes on. It is totally OK to stop and sit with it when we must.

Though your own "rash of grief" may be newly dark and painful, or perhaps a bit faded like mine, the internal scars and ongoing pain from it will probably never totally leave you. Do what you must to take care of your pain, and don't worry about the way you "look" to anyone but yourself.

Though I didn't ask for my purple spotted rash, I now wear it like a cape. It's not part of my daily outfit but something I keep close by and put on when I see someone else reeling from their own loss and grief. Instead of using my cape as a shield of self-protection or allowing it to push me away from others, I open it up and gently wrap the warmth and caring of *someone who understands* around the shoulders of those who need to know they are not alone.

In truth, your rash of grief can make you an even more unique person than before. In time, it can become like a beautiful garment just as mine has, especially if you can allow it to open your heart, increase your compassion and deepen your connection with those around you. In time, *everyone* will know what it's like to have one. Most will be grateful when you wear - and share - the warmth and comfort from it with them.

Note: It's a long story as to why they raised me, but essentially, my mother's parents stepped in when both my parents were clearly unable to manage a new-born baby. Thank God they did or mine might be the tale of grief of a very different kind. I stayed with my grandparents until they passed away. I was so blessed!

Don't tell me the moon is shining; show me the glint of light on broken glass.

Anton Chekhov

What Not to Say to A Grieving Person

I recently read the article _7 Things Not to Say to a Grieving Person_ by Katherine Britton on Crosswalk.com. I think it covers a lot of great suggestions for what not to say to a grieving person, such as "Hey, you look sad." But still I had a few things I wanted to add.

Here are a couple of them...

_Bad: "Well at least they didn't die from _____."_

As if to say that your loss is less difficult because the person didn't have a specific illness or tragedy befall them. This kind of comment almost certainly comes from someone who is totally clueless; has never gone through the death of someone close to them; or is completely narcissistic.

Better: "I'm glad they didn't suffer (long) but I know that doesn't make your pain any easier."

_Bad: "Do you still miss _____?"_

Chances are the answer is "yes" no matter how long the person has been gone, unless they were a real a-hole, or the relationship was completely estranged. I remember back in high school being with a friend whose mother had died a few weeks earlier. We were out shopping and ran into someone he knew from school who stupidly asked this very question about his recently departed mom.

Well, duh.

We were both so shocked by such a naive question. My friend mumbled a quick, "Um yeah. Thanks for asking," before we dashed away to discuss her idiotically hurtful comment.

Better: "It's great to see you."

However, probably *one of the worst things to say to a grieving person is NOTHING.* In all honesty, most people who are hurting so deeply from the loss of a loved one are barely registering much of what is going on around them. They are in a painful, hazy, mind-numbing fog in which everything is upside down and they are just trying to make sure their feet are on the ground.

If you don't know what to say, here are a few of my suggestions:

- Send them a card

- Give them a hug

- Make them laugh

- Invite them to a movie -- or bring over a movie

- Send them their favorite flowers

- Surprise them with their favorite takeout

- Chocolate, brownies, ice cream, etc.

- Get them a massage, facial or pedicure

- Better yet, schedule a spa day together

- Take them to the park

- Offer to walk their dog

- Mow their lawn

- Clean their kitchen

- Have them over for a meal

- Take them a meal

- Ask them to share a funny story or memory about their loved one

- Listen…just listen

Whatever the case, just say or do *something* to let them know you care and are there. Words of comfort are nice and appreciated but your *presence and actions* will be what they remember most - unless you are like the clueless girl above. Then you're sure to never be forgotten.

Friendship improves happiness and abates misery, by the doubling of our joy and the dividing of our grief.

Marcus Tullius Cicero

We are not here to curse the darkness, but to light the candle that can guide us thru that darkness to a safe and sane future.

John F. Kennedy

Have an Ice Day!

Recently I realized that for all her faults, my mother is responsible for introducing me to one of the greatest loves in my life – figure skating. She was an ice skater while growing up and a skating judge (figures) later in life.

Beth LOVED skating with every cell of her body. As a child, she skated on Edgemont Pond near her home in Montclair, New Jersey, and dreamed of skating professionally in Ice Follies. Though she didn't end up being in a show, she did become a figure judge for the United States Figure Skating Association (USFSA). This means she graded skaters on various types of figure eights they performed. If they passed all the maneuvers in that level, they earned badges and were allowed compete in figures at that level in competitions.

Note: Personally, I always hated doing "figures." Patch class was a skating session in which you got your own patch of ice for an hour or so. During this endless stretch of time, you had to skate figure eights on various edges (forward-inside, forward-outside, back-inside, back-outside, and various combinations of each) and was absolute torture to me, save for that it was on the ice. It was SO boring, especially since skaters weren't allowed to talk to each other during the class.

But my mother ADORED figures, perhaps even more than all the jumping and spinning I preferred. And her passion for the sport as a whole was so big that after I was born, she was determined to make sure my first word was "skate." Although that didn't happen, she did instill in me a love for the ice at a very early age.

On the one and only vacation my mother and I ever took together, we went to New Jersey. Her best friend, Dean, was skating in Ice Capades. The show was in Atlantic City, NJ for a long period at the start of the tour, so Dean had an apartment there and we went to stay with him.

Over the course of the week, we went to the beach, took a side trip to NYC, visited Montclair (including Edgemont Pond) and went to see the show. The highlight of the experience for me was getting to go back stage and meet recent Olympic gold-medalist, Dorothy Hamill - pictured on the next page.

Though I initially took lessons when I was four years old, I started skating regularly a year or so after that trip with my mom. I loved it immediately and from then on, I spent part of nearly every day at one rink or another. From skating almost daily to avidly following national and world competitions, my world was infused with figure skating through my late teens. I competed and performed too, dreaming of joining Ice Capades or Holiday on Ice.

Unfortunately, when I was fourteen, I got a severe case of mononucleosis which would not go away despite weeks of rest and anti-biotics. Eventually I had to stop skating and competing because I kept having relapses from over-exertion. It was heart-breaking.

But I couldn't stay away from the ice and soon got a part-time job at the rink. Though I started low on the totem pole, after several years, I began teaching skating until the rink closed when I was eighteen. I have no doubt part of the reason I love teaching is because of the awesome experiences I had sharing my passion with others on the ice.

About six months after the rink closed, I auditioned for *Disney on Ice,* but was evidently ten pounds too heavy for their requirements. They told me to come back when I lost it (I never lost it, so I never went back) so my skating career pretty much came to a close. Though I'd practice here and there when time allowed, I drifted away from it for quite some time, a very bitter sweet parting.

Two funny facts about this pic:

#1 Over the years, MANY people have seen this photo and asked me if Dorothy was my mom.

#2 My hair is *supposed* to be the same hair cut as Dorothy's. All the *Short & Sassy* shampoo in the world couldn't make it look like hers. Believe me, I tried!

Last weekend, my husband and I attended the United States Figure Skating Championships right here in Greensboro, NC. Though this is the second time our fair city has hosted the event, growing up I could have never imagined a major skating event - let alone Nationals - happening here.

But it did - and it was fantastic! I got to see some of my skating idols past and present including Tanith Belbin, one of the most beautiful ice dancers ever, and met a few of the up and coming stars of the sport.

As I watched one competitor after another take the ice and give their all in the hopes of a medal, I imagined my mom sitting up in the rafters of the coliseum enjoying the show.

Though I remorsefully remarked a few times to my husband and in-laws how I was not allowed to pursue the kinds of competitions which lead to Nationals, I think my mom was just trying to make sure I never lost my love for skating by getting caught up in the drama machine that comes with it. Perhaps she knew I'd get my feelings hurt too easily, or worried I'd grow to hate the sport I loved so much if I had to take it too seriously.

Whatever the case, whatever her motivation, I am so thankful to her for introducing me to skating as a child. If there is a heaven, my mom's personal slice of it has a garden on one side and an ice rink on the other, with lots of cats in-between for her to love and pet. I hope that by supporting the sport and watching the competitions, I am somehow bringing her some joy and satisfaction too.

It's been quite a few years since being on the ice was part of my daily routine (flying camels may be meant for fourteen-year-olds more so than forty+ year-olds!), I still skate in my mind and my dreams as often as I can.

It's like a moving meditation for me – there's something so calming and Zen-like in moving across the ice alone in my thoughts and the crisply cool air. Skating is still something I love and follow more than the average person. And it never would have been that way if it weren't for my mom.

Thank you, Mom, for putting a deep love of the ice - and everyone on it - in my blood. See if you can pull some strings from up above to help bring Nationals back to Greensboro again soon!

Everybody has to deal with tough times. A gold medal doesn't make you immune to that. A skater is used to falling down and getting up again.

Dorothy Hamill

*We don't receive wisdom;
we must discover it for
ourselves after a journey
that no one can take for us
or spare us.*

Marcel Proust

Finishing Unfinished Business with of Forgiveness

I'm not one to hold a grudge. Really, I'm not. In fact, I can honestly say I am still on speaking terms with just about every single ex-boyfriend I've had. True, there are a few that I haven't seen in a while. But if we ran into each other, a pleasant conversation could be had with most.

Perhaps this is because I have always been one who has loved others easily, especially those I've been romantically involved with. I tend to think it's because I have an infinitely loving spirit who sees the bigger picture, the purpose (or real person) behind the pain, and the silver lining in most situations. I am also one to forgive, forget and move on - or so I like to think.

> *To be wronged is nothing, unless you continue to remember it.*
>
> *Confucius*

Still, there are people I need to forgive for pain which came from our past relationships or interactions - and they are not former paramours per se. Some are business connections, others are family members, a few are (former) friends or romantic relations. And for the most part, the only place I see them is in my head...when I think about the past.

As someone who constantly encourages people to live from a place of love; to accept and forgive others; and to walk their talk, I've recently been faced with the tasks of doing these things myself with some folks who have hurt me deeply. And it's been something of a challenge.

But, if nothing else I am a person of action who fully believes in both karma and the powerful energy behind letting go of what you don't want to make room for what you do. I've taken a few baby steps towards mending the remaining cracks in my heart. It's time to let go of the yucky bonds of hurt which remain and embrace these folks with LOVE.

Here are a few little things I've done to begin forgiving those I need to and which you might want to try:

- Accepted their Facebook friend request or interacted with them on social media

- Used an item or object that they gave me - and not for target practice

- Prayed for them

- Thanked them (in my head or on paper*) for the insights I've gained through our relationship

- Thanked them (in my head or on paper*) for being a teacher/helping me learn

- Said out loud, "<Insert name>, I forgive you for_____."*

- Opted NOT to tell the story of how they hurt me *one more time*

- Told the story of how we hurt each other from an observer's point of view

- Sent them love, loving kindness, positive energy or thoughts of forgiveness from my heart

- Pictured them smiling and happy

- Thought about of a good memory of us or them

- Asked (in my head or on paper*) for them to forgive me

- Forgiven myself for my actions, reactions and in-actions in our relationship and past

*Some of this has been done digitally/online. At some point and if it will make things better, I hope to gain the courage to do this directly or in person, at least for the ones who are alive.

Interestingly, information about forgiveness is all around me these days in what I'm reading, seeing online and in conversations I've had. Here's an example and quote from the book *Unfinished Business* by James van Praagh. It's one of the best books I've read lately about letting go of worry, pain and old baggage:

"Failures can be seen as the opportunities you had to demonstrate love, compassion, and forgiveness to yourself and others, but choose not to follow through on."

If you are reading this perhaps it's because you too are on a path of forgiveness. Begin by forgiving and loving yourself in all the ways you can. Then make the effort to LET GO of the pain which binds you to the past and MOVE ON, with or without those who have hurt you, into a much brighter - and lighter - world.

One part of wisdom is knowing what you don't need any more and letting it go.

Jane Fonda

Refreshing the View

Over the last few weeks, I've been on a mission to make my house feel more like my *home*. Though I've lived here for more than ten years, this house has not felt as welcoming to me as I would like. This is partially due to my own lack of doing more to make it my own, as well as a number of remainders/ and reminders there was once another woman here, my husband's first wife.

Though I don't have any fear of her returning or being a threat to my marriage, Number One's style and mine are different. Additionally, a number of the artistic items displayed in this house were gathered on trips she and my husband took together when they were married. Dave never felt the need to take them down and I guess I've just felt too shy to speak up.

Then I went to stay with Jesse and Joanna - good friends of mine who live and LOVE* (**L**ive **O**n **V**acation **E**veryday) in Florida. They aren't actually on vacation - they just enjoy life like they are! Every nook of their house felt comforting, loving, welcoming and relaxing.

I found myself wanting to sit in every chair, experience every corner, and honestly, just move in. But since that kind of move would create a rather long-distance commute for both my business and marriage, I thought it wiser to try and replicate some of that snuggly feel here.

Since I got home, I've been making a few adjustments of my attitude and environment...adding a few flameless candles and lamps, cleaning out closets, and getting more organized. And though I haven't taken any before and after pictures to show the huge difference in changes, I am amazed at the energy and power created by simply taking down an old, window treatment I hated and replacing it with a beautiful sheer I love.

I'm not done - new paint, towels and light fixtures are coming to this bathroom in the near future. I also expect other parts of my house to get similar treatment one area at a time until every room feels like one I want to be in.

To me, the process and results have truly been refreshing to my spirit. Surrounding myself with such an environment is a fairly simple way to be loving to myself every day. I hope it inspires you to do the same!

We are what we see. We are products of our surroundings.

Amber Valletta

Pulling Down Whatever Blocks Your Vision

Over the last few days, I've been feeling a little overwhelmed, blocked, stressed, and a bit nervous. I've got a BIG project underway at my massage practice - an expansion - which is REALLY exciting and also a little scary at the same time. There are a lot of moving parts and things to do and has all come about very fast. I know it will be awesome as it all comes together but right now it is a little too much.

I'm not going to talk about all of the what's, whys and how's of the expansion at the moment though. Instead I want to talk about blocks - and how I get rid of them - because that is what I did all day today.

Well, I ripped ivy off of my front porch, actually. But it's pretty much the same thing. Let me explain.

Over the years, I've found when I feel blocked or stressed in one area of my life, the healthiest thing I can do is to focus on some unrelated project like cleaning, gardening, or weeding. In particular, I do well with getting rid of things, purging items I no longer need, or cleaning up spaces that are cluttered. I also like ripping ivy from my yard and house. Not sure why this helps - maybe it is a symbolic gesture of unblocking something...anything...to get the energy around me moving and clearing some of my other blocks in the process.

So yesterday, after listening to one of my favorite tapping experts, Brad Yates, and going through a particular tapping process on removing blocks, I vehemently declared as I tapped on my collar bones that I was ready to get rid of *anything* that was blocking me from moving forward on one of my specific career goals.

Then last night I had an epiphany. *The overgrown ivy around my front porch has been preventing me from moving forward and achieving success on my goals. It had to go!*

You may laugh at this idea - my husband does - but the look, feel and energy of the ivy weighs me down, makes my skin crawl and makes me feel claustrophobic. Though I admire its will to survive and thrive, I don't like how ivy can and will choke out everything around it and takeover a garden or house if allowed to. It damages or runs over almost everything in its path and knows no boundaries. Today, I actually had to pull it out from inside the soffit panels, gutter and off the roof!

As I clipped and pulled each strand of the vines away from the bricks and patio railing, I could feel myself breathing easier. Suddenly, light and air were flowing around the porch - even the house seemed to breathe a big sigh of relief. AHHHH!

But what I really loved most about getting rid of this evil creeper was immediately I could SEE everything so much more clearly. Opening up this space not only gave me a better view of my yard instantly, but it created some space in my mind to visualize the possibilities not only for the yard and house, but also my life and business. IT STOPPED CHOKING MY VISION. Removing the ivy also helped me take a dark corner where everything seemed hazy and turn it into a bright airy place of rest, reflection and peace.

For many of us, in the overgrown schedules of our lives, it is sometimes hard to find that kind of contemplative place in our minds and physical spaces. Yet if we are to accomplish our most important tasks and goals, we need have time and a place to time to rest and renew ourselves in the fresh air and sun; to have moments and places where we can contemplate the possibilities and get a fresh view of the big picture; to feel free enough to move in the direction of our passions and successes. We all need to pull down the overgrown ivy and other weeds from our lives from time to time.

When you are feeling stuck, stressed or blocked in some part of your world, I encourage you to think about another and perhaps unrelated area of your life which affects you the way the ivy affects me. Then get out your pruning shears and start tackling it one vine at a time. Soon you'll have the space to think clearly, breathe easier and see the way to success in other areas of your life.

I've learned that fear limits you and your vision. It serves as blinders to what may be just a few steps down the road for you. The journey is valuable, but believing in your talents, your abilities, and your self-worth can empower you to walk down an even brighter path. Transforming fear into freedom - how great is that?

Soledad O'Brien

Filling Each Other's Cups

Over the weekend, one of my massage clients told me about a recent experience she had at a baby shower. Rather than having a traditional shower, her friend who already has another child - and subsequently most of the baby items she really needed - was given a Blessingway or " Mother's Blessing" instead. (Read more about this Navajo tradition in *Blessingway - What Is A Blessingway?* by Kelly Winder)

At the event, attendees do things to support and honor the mother like writing poems, saying prayers, creating some kind of keepsake like a bracelet or blanket for her and/or participating in other meaningful activities. These items and actions help to connect the mother to her friends during this special time and beyond, clearly affirming each of their importance to her and her growing family.

Though I am not a mother nor expecting to be one, the idea of a blessingway immediately made me think of my growing wellness center and the amazing team of people who work with me. In a way, they are all like my kids as well as supportive friends who have helped me as I have given birth to this business. They are also creating and nurturing their own smaller parts of this enterprise, and we all are supporting each other.

As the article referenced says, "There is also so much focus on the new arrival and excitement of meeting the baby, and very little focusing on and nurturing the mother – 'filling her cup' – so it overflows with love. A woman who is given lots of love has more love to give in return..."

Like mothers, many of us, especially women and those who are care-givers like massage therapists, tend to put the focus on others so much they forget about themselves. I can attest to the fact that people who are busy growing their businesses do the same thing.

The mission and mantra at <u>my</u> wellness spa are "To create a place of healing for all who walk through our doors" and "Love our clients." In the process of growing this and other businesses, it has become quite clear to me that everyone in my business, just like mothers, are better able to fulfill our mission if our own cups are overflowing. In fact, this is true for everyone.

While we may not have the benefit of a blessingway given by others, we can and must make self-care and self-induced cup-filling a priority. Though we all have outside demands, whatever we can do to love and nourish ourselves will allow us to better nurture those we choose to mother and support. And that is a blessing!

A Year from Now You'll Wish You Started Today

Last night I started to edit a book I have been working on for the last few years, *Zen Versus Zin,* which documents my year of quitting drinking. While editing the draft, I ran across this quote from Karen Lamb which I found really powerful when I first saw it:

"A year from now you will wish you had started today."

Somewhere else I once heard the idea that if you started writing just a page a day, in one year you'd have a book of 365 pages. I've come really close to doing that as my first draft has 346 pages. Seeing the quote again made me happy to have accomplished so much on that book - and so many other things in that year and since.

One of the biggest things I've done is simply being truer and kinder to myself in all I do. I've made better choices, stopped being so hard on myself, and reframed a lot of the goals I have for my life. As a result of all of these - as well as ridding the habit of daily drinking from my life - I am much calmer, fulfilled and definitely a lot happier.

I want to encourage you to think about something - ANYTHING - that you've been wanting to start. Whether you've considered starting a diet or learning to paint; going back to school or moving to a new city; writing a book or letting go of a relationship...the time to get started on that daydream or life-long goal is NOW!!

- Imagine how GOOD you will feel a year from today when you can see all the progress or changes you've made!

- Think about what an inspiration you will be to those around you and yourself!

- Visualize how your life could be different and more engaging, fulfilling or rewarding

Choose something you feel passionate about and really want to do. WRITE IT DOWN and then underneath it, make a list of at least three small things you can do to get started on it this week. This could be as simple as doing some online research about the city you want to move to or cleaning out an overflowing drawer to make space for something new to come into your life. Pick one of those tasks and DO IT today. Not tomorrow, not next week. NOW!

Believe me, giving up a habit like drinking that was SO MUCH a part of my life was a real challenge, as was writing about it for others to eventually see. I know whatever change you're considering is scary. I also know that YOU ARE STRONG, *powerful* and <u>more than capable</u> of doing exactly what you want and need in your life.

I believe in you and know YOU are going to accomplish something special by this time next year!

How does a project get to be a year behind schedule? One day at a time.

Fred Brooks

Creating a Life that is Big, Fat and Fabulous

I have to admit it...I have a bit of a crush. Not a romantic crush, mind you, but a professional one of sorts.

Over the last several years, I've been following Whitney Way Thore. She lives in Greensboro (my hometown) and is the star of her own reality show, _My Big Fat Fabulous Life_ on TLC. But even before her show, I was entranced by her confidence and her willingness to speak up and out about the struggles she's faced as a large, overweight - or fat - woman.

Doing so is part of her movement to empower others, in particular women, who feel marginalized because of their weight or bodies. Prior to the gig with TLC, she was doing this through her blog and a series of videos she made on You Tube. (Type in Fat Girl Dancing to find them.)

Now I'm a fan of her show. This is a big deal in my eyes, especially because I HATE - well actually DEPLORE is a better word - reality television. To me those shows always seem so stupid, fake and pointless. But in MBFFL, what you see is meaningful situations unfolding in front of you: relationships, emotions, challenges, excitement, family, and the various difficulties faced by Whitney. (There are also some beautiful scenes from around Greensboro, which is also very heartwarming for this Carolina girl.)

But what is truly _fabulous_ is the spirit and attitude with which Whitney faces it all. Her humor, courage, confidence and passion are contagious and intoxicating as is her love for herself. She inspires me in every episode.

Hence the crush:-)

Living in the same city, I've been able to meet Whitney and hope someday to get to know her as a friend. I'm sure she's got tons of fans that would like that same thing, but I hope that she'll look at me as a colleague and resource who has a common purpose in making the world a better place by inspiring people to love themselves more.

I challenge you to do what you can - today and every day - to be more loving and accepting of yourself. YOU are special, perfect and wonderful just the way you are and deserve respect and love, most especially from yourself. Take steps to make YOUR own life big, fat and, of course, fabulous!

Self-love has very little to do with how you feel about your outer self. It's about accepting all of yourself.

Tyra Banks

Self-Love is In the Air

I just read - _Curves Are Here to Stay_ by Gazelle Paulo on TheBlot.com. The article features my professional girl "crush" Whitney Thore (_My Big Fat Fabulous Life_) and some other really gorgeous women who are plus size models. Although for the most part, I don't write about weight, size or body image, I LOVE to help people find ways to empower themselves and fill their spirits with LOVE. So, in the spirit of self-love and acceptance - I want to challenge you to do something empowering and loving for yourself right now.

Deep breath....

With a pad of paper and pen, go look yourself in the mirror - any mirror - and peer upon the awesomeness that is you. Take another deep relaxing breath and allow your gaze to soften. Look at your reflection in the same way you would a sleeping child or a dear friend, with love and tenderness in your heart and eyes.

Instead of picking out any flaws or other things you want to change, notice at least one thing _you like or love about yourself today._ It could be the color or style of your hair; the shape of your eyes; how cute your toes look with a new pedicure. Focus only on these positive things and jot down every single thing you see that you like or love, leaving space to add to your list in the future. You can also add non-physical qualities or skills to your list like "my sense of humor" or "taste in clothes" and "natural ability to teach children." Don't limit yourself - find as many things you like about yourself as possible.

Once you've got your list, say these words while making eye contact with yourself in the mirror:

"I like/love myself and my {insert a favorite thing here}."

Work your way down the list, showering yourself with loving reminders about why you are such a cool, interesting, lovable person. Repeat once a day or as often as you like, especially when you need a boost of self-confidence.

Mind you, though this exercise *sounds* pretty simple, it can be a fairly big challenge at first. I've been working on positive affirmations like this for more than 20 years and I still panic just a bit inside when I do them in front of a mirror.

But that's totally OK. I'm sure you were nervous before you got your first driver's license too, but now get behind the wheel without breaking a sweat. Just like driving, with practice, it will get easier to find more about yourself to become enamored with - and your self-love will begin to grow into something else you can admire and add to your list!

It is not love that should be depicted as blind, but self-love.

Voltaire

Is "GOAL" a Four-Letter Word?

If anyone knows about achieving goals, it's Oprah. So it's no surprise to see the article, _Secrets of Happy People_ by Dawn Raffel on Oprah.com questioning a book - _Goal-Free Living_ which says having no goals allows for a faster path to happiness. The book's author, Stephen Shapiro, says by having specific goals, you can lose yourself or your essence, and, in some ways, not be as happy as if you have no goals at all. Instead, he suggests people have "aspirations" and allow themselves to wander where they like rather than sticking to a goal-driven path.

I actually like a lot of points pulled from the book but KNOW I would not have completed or achieved the many things I have if I did not have a definite and SMART GOAL (specific, measurable, achievable, realistic and time-sensitive) in mind.

One example from my own life is that as an author. Ever since I was a little girl, I _aspired_ to write and publish my own books. But it was not until after I turned forty that I was able to bring that dream into reality.

After many false starts and stops, I completed my first book after I was given an opportunity to have a free trade show booth at a conference where I was speaking. Knowing the trade show was the perfect place to launch the industry resource I had been carefully crafting for years gave me the push I needed to make it happen.

Another book, **The Sunflower Princess**, sat in my files for close to FIFTEEN years before I completed it. It's a very personal story of my journey through loss and grief, and I had a lot of anxiety tied to putting it out in the world. By setting a specific goal and committing to doing a reading from it at a local book store on October 14th - my mother's birthday - I was able to push my fears to the side and get it done in time.

How this looked as a SMART GOAL when I set it: *I will finish my book, The Sunflower Princess, and have copies ready for a book launch in Greensboro, NC by October 14, 2014.*

Specific – publish *The Sunflower Princess*

Measurable – one book published by book launch

Achievable – already written, self-publishing company lined up

Realistic –final edits done, production & delivery for event doable

Time Sensitive – by October 14, 2014

Without having an exact deadline and specific purpose for being finished, the book might still be a collection of digital files on my computer! The same could be said for many other things I have wanted to accomplish, including publishing the book you now hold.

Your aspirations and the passion you have for them must be the driving forces behind whatever goals you set. Done correctly, this critical process will help you complete the tasks needed faster and more efficiently than by simply wandering aimlessly. It will also bring you closer to doing, being or having what you want.

I'm convinced…GOAL is not a bad four-letter word. It will remain a part of my vocabulary as long as I am around. And with it in my life, the only really awful four-letter word I know – FEAR – is nearly powerless over me.

I don't focus on what I'm up against. I focus on my goals and I try to ignore the rest.

Venus Williams

There are No Mistakes

Today, I stepped out of my comfort zone by taking a class in Zentangle. Well, I say "out" of my comfort zone, but in a lot of ways it was actually pretty comfortable. In fact, compared to many soul-stretching experiences, it was downright plush and cushy!

1. It was at my wellness spa

2. At a time/day I set up

3. With an instructor I hired

4. And I was surrounded by people I already know (and like:-)

Ahh the benefits of being your own boss!

However, the act of "doing art" - and of being instructed on how to be visually artistic - is something I lost comfort with a long time ago. My talents lie in being a creative or visionary entrepreneur, a thoughtful writer, and a compassionate healing artist. Classes in any of these areas feel fresh, exciting and yet familiar at once, kind of like test driving a newer, better model of a car you already know and love. But creating visual art feels stiff, awkward and hard to snuggle up with after so much time apart.

I can't begin to explain all the issues this brought up for me - or why it did - but I found it a really interesting exercise of self-exploration and examination. You may have heard the saying before, "The way you do anything is the way you do everything," and let's just say Zentangle made some of my habits and character flaws VERY evident to me.

The biggest one, ahem, is that I am a perfectionist or idealist. I get a certain idea in my head of how I want something to be, especially things I am doing or creating, and will often want to JUST STOP once I see the thing is not going in the direction I thought it would.

I also noticed I can feel very anxious and become easily discouraged when I am on unfamiliar ground. Though I know I can overcome most anything I encounter, I heard LOTS of old tapes kick in as we learned about halos and half-moons.

- My *inner critic* said it was too hard and that my abilities were not as good as the others at the table.

- My *restless child* - the one who drops what she is holding to run after a bright shiny object in the distance - told me she was bored. She didn't like the tedious coloring in of some of the designs and wanted to do something more fun and exciting. Plus, she was hungry.

- My *busy entrepreneur* had more important things to do and could not believe I was spending *two whole hours* drawing.

- And my *perfectionist* wanted to throw away the whole thing when I accidentally overlapped two lines (upper left corner - can't even see them now) and made a few incomplete circles (in the bottom right corner).

Whew that was tiring! And there was also **a lot** more going on in my head I cannot articulate now. But I'm happy to say, at the end of it all, I was generally happy with my creations and want to do it again.

If I can share any wisdom from this experience, it would be this:

- Stay with what you start long enough to see the beauty and outcome that is possible.

- Give yourself credit for the talents you do possess.

- Let go of the negative judgments you have about yourself and accept your uniqueness.

- Stop trying to be like others and focus on being the best YOU possible.

- One step at a time, you can do more than you ever imagined.

- Others may surprise you by having different viewpoints than yours, and you can like them all.

- Despite what it may look like at the onset, there are very few "mistakes" that truly ruin the picture. In fact, "mistakes" may just be the elements that makes a particular story or picture more beautiful and special to you.

There's more to Zentangle than drawing. It's an amazing tool to create space in your mind and day where healing can occur.

Take chances, make mistakes. That's how you grow. Pain nourishes your courage. You have to fail in order to practice being brave.

Mary Tyler Moore

It's Mother's Day...again

It's Mother's Day, one of those hallmark holidays that sends scads of people in search of the perfect card or gift to let mom know "just how much she means" - and a few other mostly silent folks who are in search of a place to hide until it's over.

My mom was not a perfect mother, probably not even a good mother by any standards, especially mine. She essentially abandoned me at birth by leaving me in the care of her parents - my beloved grandparents - who were in their seventies and still working full-time as college professors (my grandfather was also a dean) at the now defunct Southwood College in eastern NC.

My mother, who was unemployed and married - also to a professor - was not able to take care of me. Though it was never discussed specifically, I suspect Beth had postpartum depression on top of her usual manic depression and other health issues and simply couldn't cope with a newborn.

Evidently her postpartum problems lasted for a really long time, and she continued to be unwilling or unable to live with me under the same roof for many years. Then, after my father died a little more than ten years later, Beth pulled it together in record time and moved in with us ASAP, most likely so she wouldn't have to pay rent anymore. She and I literally almost missed the start of my father's memorial service because we were tied up returning the moving van.

My mom and I had a few close years in between which are colored with memories of us surrounded by cats, smoking pot with her friends, and playing lots of backgammon, solitaire and gin rummy. We went to yard sales and flea markets, a few rock concerts and spent lots of time out in the garden.

And then there are the other memories which creep in and invade my mind of her various "attacks" of pain, drama, depression and guilt; the scores of prescription medicine bottles and overflowing ashtrays in her bedroom; and the frightening encounters with her scary, drunken inappropriate loser boyfriends. At times, I am still haunted by her total inability to move beyond her own past hurts and limitations to be a good mom to me.

Though we did spend a lot of time together once she moved in, doing the math now, I see that my mom and I really had a brief window of mother-daughter closeness, starting around the time my dad got sick when I was almost nine to about the time I got my first boyfriend five years later. Perhaps she was jealous of these men in my life and could only be comfortable with me when they were absent - or on the way out?

I'm being harsh, and I know it, but on days like today, Mother's Day, the cold hard reality of not having a mother worthy of most greeting cards available hits me in the face. It can't be avoided really, for everywhere you turn people are waxing poetic about how amazing their moms were or are, how they're best friends, and they couldn't imagine life without their moms by their side. I never really had to imagine what life would be like without my mom, because I've spent most of my life that way.

Before she died in 1990, my mom and I went through a pretty rough patch starting when I was fourteen or so and only resolving about a year prior to her death. Even then it was tenuous, tedious, and stressful, although we were finally making a few positive steps towards some type of meaningful relationship. But then she truly abandoned me by taking her own life, once again leaving me with the searing belief that she didn't love me - or at least not enough to be there for me and present in my life.

Whatever the case, I have done and will continue to do things to help me heal and fill in the hole left by my mother's absence as well as the many often deeper divots caused by our times together. It's a process that will take a lifetime.

In the meantime, I am forever grateful to the many women (and men) who have stepped in at one point or another to help mother, comfort and heal me - and who have been my family.

And despite what it may sound like, I am also grateful to my mother, for without all the difficulties that came from being her daughter, I wouldn't be who I am. Forgiving her is an ongoing practice and process. Writing is a part of that as is sharing my story with others who may also be missing the woman they wish their mom had been. Go do something to mother yourself or share your own mothering energy with someone else who needs it.

As for me, today, I am coping with reality and being grateful anyway.

Gratitude makes sense of our past, brings peace for today, and creates a vision for tomorrow.

Melody Beattie

Do You Defend Your Limitations?

Not long ago, I re-read one of the first inspirational books I ever picked up, *Illusions* by Richard Bach. It's an easy read about a carefree pilot who runs across an unexpected mentor as he flies around the mid-west.

Though there are many bits of wisdom in the short paperback, one of my favorite quotes in it is this one:

"Argue for your limitations, and sure enough they're yours."

As a massage therapist, I see people do this all the time. They argue for and claim their pain, diseases and dysfunction. Just today, I was recounting the story of a client who wanted me to help with her back pain by giving her a massage, yet she did not want to make one small change in the way she sat (i.e. her posture) every day to make the pain go away on a more permanent basis.

Though she seemed to understand what I was saying, she argued with me about how she liked sitting that way, even though she knew it was causing her pain to get worse. In other words, she was balking at the solution and fighting to hold onto her pain as well as the source of her "limitation." Crazy, huh?!

As a business coach, I often hear people tell me why they can't do or have something they want. Their "reasons" include not having enough money, time, experience, contacts, skills, luck, etc.

And because they so clearly see it that way, they are right. They CAN'T do, be or have what they want - not with the mindset they have now. Instead they are claiming and clinging to the problem, lack or obstacle more fiercely than the outcome they say they desire.

Makes you wonder what they really want, doesn't it?

I could give you countless examples from other areas of my life as well because *most people have adopted a set of behaviors, guidelines, handicaps or limitations that rule and shape our lives, thoughts, language and actions.*

Why do we do this?

Most likely it is the fact that staying with the familiar - even the sucky, undesirable, painful familiar - feels safer than the unknown. In our minds, sticking with something we know hurts less than the possibility of what we might encounter if we tried something new - and FAILED. We're worried the pleasure, comfort, and routine we "lose" by doing something different may be better than the result we get by changing. But what if it's not?

I'm here to tell you, as someone who faces the possibility of loss and failure day after day - whether in my business, personal life or athletic pursuits as a triathlete - these are not the worst things that can happen to you. In many cases, staying stuck in old, stagnant, painful patterns and habits is much worse, especially in the long-term.

After I started this last night, I picked up the book I'm currently reading, *The Witch of Portobello* by Paulo Coelho – one of my favorite authors - and came across this well-timed line:

"Changes only happen when we go totally against what we're used to doing."

Today I challenge you to think of one way you're limiting yourself by defending your old comfortable choices. It could be anything from always ordering the same flavor of ice cream to staying with your current job or career because it's what you've always done.

Allow yourself the freedom and creativity to think of what you might be willing to try if there were no risk involved and if you were sure there could be no downside or negative consequences. Find a way to argue for an unfamiliar choice or change that you want to make.

Make a list of reasons why you could or should something new. What habits could you stop to improve your health, increase your finances or free up your time to make a bigger change?

Let's try a simple change on for size...

Example: *I always order butter pecan ice cream.*

What I would try if there was no risk: *cookie dough*

Why I should try it: *I really liked cookie dough as a child.*
I've seen other people get this flavor and they seem to like it.
It's just ice cream. I can afford to try something new.

Ideas which reduce the risk of trying it:
I bet I could even get a free sample at the ice cream shop. Maybe my friend will try it with me and split the cost.
Perhaps the family could have an ice cream tasting for fun and would could each try something new.

New mindsets:
I can still get butter pecan if I don't like the new flavor as much.
I'm excited about an ice cream adventure.

Stop arguing for the familiar and begin making a case for doing something totally different. Open your mind to the possibility that by getting lost or making a mistake, you might learn something new about yourself, discover a new skill or unearth a hidden treasure.

Let go of the habit of worrying about the potential loss and failure and believe doing something you previously thought was impossible might just be the way to the life or path you've been looking for.

We all have things that limit us and that challenge us. But really, our real limitations are the ones we believe.

Amy Purdy

In Order to Win, You Have to Show Up!

Over the weekend, I had a chance to meet some young athletes who visited my wellness spa. They were in town for the *New Balance Track Championships* competing in the Relay Medley Event.

In passing, one of the girls wondered aloud what would happen if their team finished last. I told her a bit about my own experience with triathlons - see *My First Top 3 Finish* for another musing on triathlons and "placing" at an event. What matters most is that you show up and start.

When I got home, I remembered I'd previously written something else about tris and looked through my files to find this, written August 20, 2011. I know a lot of people don't believe I ever lack for confidence, so I wanted to share this to as a way to show how I pump myself up to do the tough stuff. Enjoy!

*****

It's the eve of my first triathlon, the <u>Ramblin' Rose</u> in Winston Salem, NC. My event training is done, gear bought, schedule and pre-event meal planned.

This afternoon I will go to pick up my registration packet, attend a pre-event clinic on how to set up my transition area and scout out the biking and running courses. Then I'll go home to gather my thoughts, pack for tomorrow and relax with friends for a few hours before heading to bed.

But I've gotta be honest…I'm really kind of nervous. Well, nervous in a confident sort of way. I understand the set-up and sequence of events. I've got directions to the event location and a checklist for what I need to take tomorrow printed out.

Perhaps most importantly, I know I can do each of the required segments since did a practice triathlon earlier this week – albeit with the elements spread apart over several hours unlike how they'll be tomorrow. I completed about seventy-five percent of the overall distance I'll do in the real event. Yay me!

And though I was really tired after my practice tri, I woke up the next day with almost no soreness or fatigue (until I took a Zumba and yoga class later that day.) Thus, I rewarded myself and got rid of the soreness with a fantastic massage on my legs and upper shoulders. I've already got one set up for the day after the event and am as stoked about getting that massage as I am about completing this athletic milestone.

So why am I nervous? *Because I've never done anything like this before.* True, I used to compete in figure skating events as a teen and pre-teen. I've participated in a number of cycling events of twenty to forty miles each. And, at 41, I'm probably in the best shape and conditioning of my adult life - thanks to all my recent training.

But this is different.

This is pushing my physical abilities and envelope in a completely new way. I'm combining two activities – running and biking – both of which I enjoy and do fairly well with another in which I am a complete novice. Gulp...swimming.

It's not that I didn't know how to swim before now – it's just that I didn't like to. My first memory of swimming was of taking group lessons as a toddler. I was fairly shy and afraid of both the water and the teacher. When I wouldn't jump in on my own, her solution was to push off the diving platform, which scared me even more. That was the last lesson with her!

Even though I successfully learned to swim through private swimming lessons the next year, I've nearly always felt awkward and anxious in a pool or other body of water, save for one summer I spent with my cousins in Wisconsin (almost thirty years ago). During that trip, I went to the pool and swam every single day but have barely been in a pool since.

A few years later, I had a very scary experience in the ocean. My boyfriend and I were at the beach during the late summer. Though I was still nervous in the water, I felt somehow safer with him there and tried body surfing. We weren't too far out, but still further than I'd ever been from the shore.

Though it was fun at first, I didn't know how to predict the waves movement or strength very well and had a few bad wipe outs. Coming up from one of them and being a bit unaware, I was smacked down hard and got disoriented under the water. I couldn't tell up from down and swam down towards the sand as my air ran short. When I finally made my way to the top, I was gasping for air, sucking in seawater as yet another wave hit me. I was terrified.

Since then, I've had recurrent and vivid nightmares about drowning. Sometimes I've been alone and other times I've had sharks around me (another fear) but in all of them I've been unable to breathe or get to the surface. Thus, my swimming efforts and abilities have receded more and more as has my desire to improve them.

Until now.

As the deadline for event registration got closer and closer, I knew I had to push myself past my fear of the water and swimmer's ear to be able to participate. I put it off testing the waters time and time again but began taking baby steps into the shallow end of the pool a few weeks ago.

First, I called local indoor pools to find out their hours and prices for adult swimming. I posted messages on Facebook about needing a swim coach and watched swimming instructional videos on YouTube. I made a trip to a local tri-athlete supply store and bought ear plugs, a swim cap, and nose clip (you never know). Finally, I visited and joined a gym with a pool – and dove in.

Sadly, that first swim brought all my fears and goals into clear view. My freestyle stroke and related breathing abilities were sub-par and not good enough to get me across the pool once, let alone all 225 yards I'd have to swim at the Ramblin' Rose. I gasped, choked and panicked within moments of taking the water. Immediately crushed, I thought my chances of completing the live event tomorrow – or any triathlon - was totally out of reach.

Then I remembered someone telling me they had done the back stroke in a similar sprint triathlon earlier this year. As with all the other swimming techniques, I hadn't done the back stroke in years but thought maybe it was worth a try.

I went back to the side of the pool, grabbed the edge and pushed off in a backward glide across the water. I started pulling myself across one stroke at a time, working to establish some kind of a rhythm between my arms, legs and breathing. It was a struggle at first, mostly because I was upset and trying a bit too hard.

But suddenly I was at the other end of the lane and realized I might actually be able to pull this off. I pushed off again, relaxed a little and got into cadence that felt pretty good. Soon was across the pool again and back to where I began. Within fifteen minutes, I completed 250 yards and knew I could do so again. Just five days later, I combined my new ability with a bike and run. Woo hoo!

I don't know exactly how tomorrow's event will go, but I know I can finish it. I am excited to enjoy and savor each part of the day – from packing my gear and setting up my transition area to chatting in line with other novice swimmers to riding my bike and running through beautiful downtown Winston Salem on an unseasonably cool August morning. I'm excited to hear my husband cheering for me as I swim, pedal and jog past him and to feel the cool air and warm sun on my damp body and hair. And yes of course, I am eagerly anticipating crossing the final finish line, discovering my overall time and heartily celebrating the completion of the race.

But regardless of how things turn out tomorrow, what place I finish in or whether everything goes well or less than perfectly, I know *I've already won.* I've challenged myself over and over during my training to try new things and "swim" out of my comfort zone while facing and embracing my fears.

And as I've striven for excellence athletically, I've also achieved greater things in other areas of my life, especially my career. The level of focus and commitment required to be ready for this event has been transferred to my business which has already brought some huge rewards. I am blessed.

Most importantly, I've gotten more comfortable with who I am, what I am capable of doing and what I envision for my future.

I am proud of and confident myself in a way I've never been before. To me, that is more important than anything else, especially how I place in a race. (That and getting my victory massage on Monday:-)

So yes, no matter how it goes or how long it takes, I have won the race by getting this far and doing what it takes to finish tomorrow. I know I can do it!

*****

Congratulations to the girls from Westfield, and everyone who prepares for and starts at any race or event that has pushed them the way doing triathlons has pushed me. We are all winners!

My First Top 3 Finish

A lot of success in life and business comes just by showing up. I mean certainly, there's training, preparation, education, planning and all that. But at the end of it all, none of those will matter if you don't take action and SHOW UP!

Yesterday, for the first time ever, I earned the distinction of placing in the Top 3 in my age group at a local triathlon! The event, Tri for Hospice, raised money for our local Hospice organization, a charity my business supports throughout the year in different ways. When I found out about the event just a week ago, I was pretty unsure I was ready to take part.

I've been training for an event next month but am not in top form yet. Although I've been running a lot for the last few months and feel really good in that area, I just started back with my swim coach last week.

We've modified a few things about my position in the water which has my swimming in a bit of disarray and I'm still working the kinks out. Though I have a recumbent bike at home which I've used a lot, I've also been lazy about getting on my road bike, and the two are just not the same.

I have no excuse other than it's hard to do everything needed between running my businesses and trying to have a small social life. But after some thought – and the unexpected chance to become a sponsor of the event – I decided to dive in, literally, as of two days before the triathlon.

I have to be honest and tell you, I almost didn't do it. In addition to my lack of adequate training, I was not feeling my best when I woke up yesterday.

My real pre-race meal the night before included some crab dip which did not quite agree with me. In fact, it left me feeling so nauseous I couldn't have my usual pre-event breakfast.

I also had the beginnings of a poison ivy rash starting on my arms and a headache…all great reasons to stay home and go back to bed. But I'd made a commitment to myself and to Hospice – and told A LOT of people I was doing it. So off I went and signed up as a last-minute participant at the course.

The race went well all things considered. The swim was not my best: super cold water, an unfamiliar pool, and my first event in almost two years. I felt like I slid back a bit towards being a "not-drowner" rather than being the swimmer I've worked hard to become. But I made it out alive, got my bike shoes on and donned the rest of my cycling gear before hitting the road.

The bike was better – it is my best area usually – but as I said, I hadn't been on my road bike **at all** since last summer. Still I slogged through ten miles feeling pretty comfortable and then had to face the two-mile run. The course was what I feared it would be – a lot of rolling hills, most of the steepest up-hill parts coming on the way to the finish.

As I trotted along the first mile of the run, I passed a guy about my age, Murphy, who was walking down the hill. I recognized him from the bike route where I'd passed him changing a flat tire on his bike.

"You know this means the way back will be almost all up-hill, right?" I said as I slowly jogged past him.

"I almost feel guilty for walking the easy part," he replied with a bit of a frown on his face. I told him it wasn't about perfection, that it simply was about finishing the race and he shouldn't worry about anything else.

"Three months ago, I was on the cardiac ward," Murphy responded. "I just want to finish even if I come in last."

Stunned yet impressed, I said, "Then you need to just be proud of yourself for being here and be glad you're still breathing. Even if you finish last, you're ahead of all the people who didn't show up today."

We continued on to banter a bit more before I ran ahead of Murphy, thinking how lucky we both were to be there. He finished a few minutes behind me and I cheered him on as he crossed the finish line. We both watched and clapped as they gave awards out to the top 3 overall finishers and the #1 finishers in each age group. Then we both packed up our gear and went our separate ways.

I didn't see my results until I got home later and saw that I placed in the Top 3 in my age group. I was thrilled to hit such an accomplishment on my first race of the year and without being truly prepared for it.

But here's the funny part...*there were only three people in my age group.* And yet I'm still happy about being in the Top 3:-)

Why? Though a lot of folks don't realize it, many athletes and professionals do "well" simply because they just show up when others won't. They are one of the best in their niche or field because they are willing to step out, take a risk, try something new or simply BE THERE when others aren't.

Just showing up to attempt to conquer a difficult task or goal is much more than many people will even consider, let alone do.

If triathlons have taught me nothing else, it is that being there and being willing to do your best, regardless of the "perceived" outcome or "place" you achieve – or the possible failure you might experience – makes you achieve success more often.

I am quite happy with my "top 3" finish. I showed up, even when I didn't feel my best or most confident. Yes, I was afraid of failure, and of looking stupid, and had a few other things stacked against me. But I took a deep breath as I made the first step into the icy cold pool and persevered to the last step as I ran across the grassy finish line. By doing just that, both Murphy and I – along with all of the participants of the race – finished on top:-)

Special thanks to Murphy for inspiring me to share this story.

Showing up is not all of life - but it counts for a lot.

Hillary Clinton

When the Cure is Worse Than the Illness

I already know my thoughts here are going to cause some people, or at least one person, to step back and judge me. That's OK, because we all have our own perspective from which we see life and evaluate everything. Her perspective is edgy and bluntly opinionated while mine is fiercely compassionate and ever open-minded, at least when it comes to the big picture of the definition of healing. But she'll probably never read this, so here goes.

Others -including you - will simply not read it because it is too hard, too emotional, too raw. That's OK too. You are where you are.

All that being said, it's hard to know where to start. I'm at a period in my life where I've got the opportunity to reexamine a lot of things I thought I knew about myself, particularly the parts my history related to my mom. It was a tough time with her, and in truth, sometimes just writing the word "mom" causes a pain in my heart because it is so much more familiar and loving than talking about "my mother."

It's a long story, some of which I've written about before. Suffice it to say here that my mom had severe mental illness which caused a lot of problems, heartache and feelings of abandonment for me as a kid and still today. She died almost twenty-five years ago from suicide - a prescription drug overdose - and I am now at the age she was when she and I first began to spar and tangle the way teenagers and parents often do.

Add hormone-fueled rebellion and teenage angst to a relationship where severe depression/bi-polar disorder/possible multiple personality disorder exists and it's a real recipe for combustion and conflict. Thus, recovering from her death as well as all the turbulence that came before it has been a long road.

One of the key things I've learned about depression and mental illness is that often it comes to people who are unusually talented, intelligent and often, geniuses. My mother, despite all her flaws, was a gifted musician and played numerous instruments. The piano was her true love and she was classically trained - but she also played the flute, French horn, violin, viola, cello and organ. Additionally, she was very skilled in needlepoint, crocheting, knitting and had a bright green gardener's thumb. I got none of these talents.

The daughter of two college professors, and wife of another, she was articulate, witty and a great writer. Just recently, I ran across something she wrote about being diagnosed late in life with epilepsy - a diagnosis I am not sure I believe. Even after years of smoking pot, drinking and abusing multiple prescription medications - after a massive heart attack, multiple hospitalizations, shock treatment and at least one other drug overdose that I know of, her words were succinct, eloquent and extremely well-organized. I was taken aback to say the least and reminded of just what a tragedy it was that she suffered so much.

So how in the world does all this background relate to healing or to the cure being worse than the illness?

First, I stumbled across this article by on HighExistence.com, thanks to someone who seems to disagree with enough of it that she's chosen to make fun of it via social media: _Rethinking Mental Illness: Are We Drugging Our Prophets and Healers?_

I won't go into the article too much - you can read it if you want. I'll just say that a lot of it resonated with me because of my mom, the journey I've seen others in my life go through with depression, and my own experiences.

Though I tried a number of medications, I ultimately chose to fight through my own depression without antidepressants because the side effects of each drug I tried were not acceptable to me. One pill, which seemed to work pretty well at making me feel normal inconveniently gave me suicidal thoughts. That was definitely not an improvement!

Others left me feeling cloudy, groggy, or a shadow of my creative, energetic, passionate self. They also killed my libido which was not good for my marriage. There was one drug which actually worked very well in terms of making me feel like myself with no suicidal thoughts. However, it caused my hair to fall out, which caused me a completely different level of depression and anxiety.

I also tried tons of herbal supplements which are supposed to help depression. No bad side effects but none of them helped either. Thus, I gave them up too and now take nothing beyond the occasional half a Xanax when I am experiencing extreme anxiety.

Note: Years later, I found - quite by accident - that drinking alcohol regularly, even in seemingly modest amounts, was a huge trigger for my depression. This fact alone has made it relatively easy for me to stay the fairly new course of being a non-drinker.

In my case, the truth of the matter is that medication for depression did not help me become a better "me." If anything, it muted down my brightest hues and added unnecessary distractions and problems to my life. While I can't say depression is what has made me a good massage therapist or a "healer," it has given me a huge well of compassion for others who are in pain. In its' deep abyss, I have also had immense creativity, especially in the form of writing but also in my businesses, as well as huge leaps in personal growth and my own healing.

The second reason I am prompted to write is a friend who has been struggling to fight cancer - and is now at the end of his life. As he is my husband's friend rather than mine, I have spent much of this journey through diagnosis and treatment as an observer only. Like many in our society, Byron chose to turn much of his power and treatment over to traditional western doctors and medicine, enduring round after round of chemo and then radiation.

As I've listened to him share details about the treatments and effects - first positive, then negative – I've become more and more certain given the same diagnosis and choices, I would probably not accept these harsh and toxic "therapies." Looking back from where Byron is now, basically on his deathbed and just about two years since he was diagnosed, I'm even more sure of that choice. For as his health has declined over the last few months, it seems clear the "medicines" which were supposed to help him - have been as detrimental to him as the disease itself, if not more so.

How is that healing?

Dying from cancer is no picnic, obviously. But dying from cancer when your taste buds have been fried into malfunctioning and you can't eat anything sweet or salty seems extraordinarily cruel. Losing the ability to walk without pain or feel things with your hands and feet to an ever-worsening neuropathy and severe lymph edema is an unjust end to an already too short life. Watching someone's hair and teeth drop out as their life ebbs away is simply heartbreaking.

Maybe these treatments allowed Byron the time to see people he wouldn't have otherwise and do things he couldn't have without them. We'll never know. But I wonder if what these "healing" poisons have taken from him is greater.

From my perspective, these "cures" are far worse than the illness. While my body's own healing resources and attitude alone might not be enough to cure me from depression or other illnesses I've had, I can't imagine putting myself through what Byron has if I had cancer. Beyond exploring every natural alternative I could find, as I have with my depression, I think I'd choose to live a potentially shorter yet natural life in which I could keep more of ME - the physical, mental and emotional - intact.

If there's anything good that can come from Byron's illness, and from my mom's, maybe it is the cracking open of my understanding and the ability to see that for me there is another path other than what they chose. Perhaps my words will be a prompt which causes you to find ways be gentle with yourself in all ways, especially as you work to heal and "cure" your own problems and issues.

Whether it is for your mental, emotional, physical or even financial health, I encourage you to seek solutions which allow you to keep and enrich your essence more fully rather than chipping away at it pill by pill.

Find nourishing treatments and tools which allow you to savor quality over quantity as you work toward healing. If we can all do that, perhaps the illnesses experienced by Byron, my mom, and even me, are stepping-stones to a greater CURE we all need and desire: a life well-lived to the last moment possible with no regrets.

Sending my deepest love and prayers for peace to Byron...and to my mom...with forgiveness.

*The art of medicine
consists in amusing the
patient while nature
cures the disease.*

Voltaire

Mother-Love and Letting Go

I'm down at the beach unexpectedly for a brief but fun girls' trip. This afternoon, as I was dipping my toes in the water, I remembered something I wrote a few months ago when I was at the beach in Melbourne, Florida. It seems like something I should share here and today, despite the fact that the trip I'm on now is a bit less reflective than that one. Anyway, I hope it helps someone out there feel a little bit better, especially those who may be struggling with their own mother-love issues.

I'm not sure when I realized it – that I was still angry with my mother. I think it came about as a part of adding "back story" to my blog and book, Zen Versus Zin. *Things I hadn't thought about – stories I've never told – and songs I'd never listened to as an adult brought with them the emotions of a young child who never felt loved enough by her mother. If it weren't for stopping drinking in that city of hers (NYC) back in March 2014, perhaps I never would have felt these feelings again.*

Over the last few weeks, I've been overcome with the idea that I am still angry. Twenty-five years since her death and ultimate abandonment - and I'm still angry. Or I was.

I've told a few people about these residual emotions – people who I trust. I've seen my mom in my thoughts or daydreams in a way I never have in the last 25 years and think she is trying to let me know she is OK.

The other day, I was driving home listening to one of her favorite songs on XM – Born to Be Alive, by Patrick Hernandez I think. In my mind's eye I could see her above me, as if she were standing on the upper level of a shopping mall - looking over the railing and smiling in that cat-eyed, closed-mouth way of hers - because I was still enjoying that song.

She was there with two of her closest friends, Dean and Frank, who both died from AIDS after she took her own life. They were all happy: happy to see each other; happy to see me remembering them and listening to disco; happy in the place where they are now.

Perhaps it was like the out-of-body experiences she used to tell me about having or doing. It made me smile to think they were all in a positive place and together again. Then once in Melbourne, I had a dream that Frank was visiting me. I don't know what he was telling me, but it was good.

This morning, after my triumphant run to the top of a nearby bridge, I decided to go to the beach. I walked on the boardwalk, enjoying the view, and was nearly ready to go back to the house when I felt an urgent need to put my bare feet in the sand. So, I grabbed my flip flops and walked out to the water.

As I walked along the shore, I saw another vision of my mother. This time, she was standing by a gate or an archway trellis leading to a door. At first, I thought she was blocking my way or waiting for me to have/do/be enough to win her love and gain access to the treasures behind the door.

I told her I was tired of the way we've been doing things, that I wasn't sure she even had access to the door, so I was going to go through it on my own. I had the key, wisdom and energy needed to open the door myself and didn't need her to do it for me.

I also thanked her for making me who I am and kissed her on the cheek as I walked by her through the door into an amazing world of rainbows and flowers and pure love. I told her I was not waiting for her anymore and that I was going to go into the place that had been closed off for so long. Perhaps I'll see her there.

Tears flowed as I got myself together and went back to the house where I stretched and visited with Joanna and her family. I told Joanna about my experience as well as a story from my childhood in which my mother may have said she didn't love me. This became a deeply healing conversation in which I thanked Joanna for being so mothering to me and for being my friend. Then she did a tarot card reading for me.

So many things came from the impromptu session, but here are the most important parts:

- *I have the key to the gate/door/future.*

- *I am not my mother although I have allowed her to haunt me through the fear that I might be like her.*

- *She is better and finally healing where she is.*

- *I have planted many seeds for success in my life and they are blooming as am I.*

- *My mother did not resonate with this world. She gardened and planted flowers to ground herself and try to bring her vibrations in tune with the planet.*

- *I am not a gardener (in the dirt) but cultivate many things in and around myself and others, especially energetically. I don't need the dirt/grounding in the way she did.*

- *My mother was an amazing gardener and I was her greatest "flower."*

- *My mother did not abandon me — I chose to leave her to be with my grandparents and/or on my own. This choice is what made me "premium" instead of "regular."*

- *I have been holding myself back to try to a) bring her along or b) punish myself for the threat of being like her.*

- *I need to stop being a martyr – taking on too much so that others may heal, grow and prosper. Now is the time for me to set the example of what it is to be the one to grow, heal and prosper.*

- *I am my own best parent.*

Today as I walked on the beach, I also saw the ocean as the mind of the world. When it is calm, everything around it is calm. When it is angry and stormy, it upsets everything else around it. The oceans of my mind need to be calm and stay clear in order for others around me and in my world to flourish. It is not my responsibility to make them flourish – that is up to them. But, like the ocean, I can help them float.

My lessons and life are as tiny in this world as a grain of sand is on the beach. Yet the power to move the entire universe and to create a new reality is in the smallest cell in my little finger. I have the power I need to get what I want – I simply must learn to harness my power through focused intention.

*****

I am grateful to be back at the beach in a place that helps me regain my focus and clarify my intentions. I encourage you to find your own ways of calming the oceans or storms in your mind, forgiving those who've hurt you and finding the love you desire in yourself. By harnessing your own deepest powers, you can do whatever is needed to change your life and make it the way you want it to be.

Note: I was in Sunset Beach, NC when I wrote this. Ironically, the last time I was there was the week my mother died in 1990.

Friendship and a Love That Lives On

Today my husband and I - along with many others - celebrated the life of Dave's best friend, Byron. Everyone who attended the beautifully casual event was invited to speak. Though he and I weren't that close, I decided to say a few words after a dream I had last night. I thought I'd share what I said here in the hopes it might bring others comfort - and so Byron's story can live on.

Hi I'm Felicia Brown. I'm married to David Clayton, who was very close friends with Byron since their time together at UNC. Since our relationship was through Dave, I probably didn't know Byron as well as many of you.

Although we've been on a few trips together over the years, and spent some time watching Carolina basketball — GO HEELS! - I wasn't the one who was "friends" with Byron...I was "the wife" of his friend. Thus, I've more often hung in the background or given the boys their time to catch up, shoot the breeze and solve the world's problems over a few good beers. Still I loved Byron for who he was and feel his loss greatly.

I wanted to speak today because I hope to help those of you who were his close friends, confidants, and family, perhaps feel a little bit better in this time of grief. Some of what I'm about to say may seem odd, but more than anything, I want you to know that you are not alone. I've been where you are.

Twenty-five years ago today, I lost my mom quite unexpectedly. Before and after that, I said a final farewell to several other close members of my family and numerous good friends. Often, soon after these folks have passed on, I've had dreams (in my sleep) in which they've come back to let me know they are OK, that they still loved me, and that I didn't need to worry about them anymore.

For weeks I've wondered if I would have such a dream about Byron. Seeing as how he and I were not that close, I thought it was unlikely, but still I've hoped.

Then last night – after a fun dinner out with some of Byron's friends and reminiscing about old times - I had a dream. I was in New York to teach at a conference – something I do once each year. I was sitting at an outdoor café reading the New York Times when I came across a half page ad for a new TV show about the adventures of five quirky and funny guys who had recently moved to New York.

Three of them were middle-aged Jewish men David and I know in Greensboro. The fourth was quite similar to Buddy G. – who, in case you don't know him, is a made-for-TV comedy special all on his own. And the main character, of course, was Byron.

In the ad, Byron was youthful, confident and happy. He was dressed like he was ready for a night out on the town, had a look of mischief on his face and a gleam in his eye. And – as a writer for the show – he was excited to tell lots of entertaining stories about the fun adventures and mishaps he was having in his new home of NYC.

I don't think you need to know much about dream analysis to see the parallel between this dream and the others I mentioned. To me it says that Byron is getting settled in his new place. He's back to being himself – feeling good and ready to take on the world. He's got new friends there, some who remind him of the ones he had here, and he's gonna keep making memories that will make people smile and laugh.

This dream - and the others like it in the past - gives me comfort. It reminds me that regardless of where Byron is now, his essence and that which we all loved about him lives on in our hearts, minds and dreams.

In closing, I'd just like to share a quote I found a few days ago which made me think of Byron, both because it was from Van Gogh, a famous Dutch artist whose work is well-showcased at the Van Gogh museum in Amsterdam, a city which he loved and considered his second home, but also for the content.

Van Gogh said:

"I tell you the more I think, the more I feel that there is nothing more artistic than to love people."

In this way, Byron was a true artist. We were all so blessed to be a part of colors he chose in the canvas of his life. Namaste.

What I really got from today and from Byron's illness and death is this reality: You get back what you put out. Byron put out unconditional love, acceptance, friendship and caring. He was loyal, funny, interested, and genuine. He made the effort to see and stay connected to people he considered his friends FOR LIFE - even when they moved to another state or country, got married, had kids, or fought cancer. As a result, there was a room full of people who each considered Byron their best friend, and he probably was exactly that to each of them.

We rarely know the kind of impact we are making on others, or how deeply we touch people's lives, until some unfortunate circumstance occurs. Today, I saw a group of people who truly loved and appreciated the person we were there to honor and remember. Byron won each of their friendships, not just because he was a part of their lives when it was easy and convenient back in the day, but also because he remained invested in the connections they'd established long after the convenience factor was gone. He was kind to a fault, compassionate, and loving with most everyone he knew.

Byron set a new bar for me to achieve in my own relationships. And wherever he is now, I hope Byron can now see what a huge impact he's had on the world. May his love and devotion LIVE ON in those missing him - and all reading this - inspiring us to deepen our relationships and stay better connected to those we truly care about...*for life.*

Buddy, Byron and Dave in Chicago

Today I Write Just for Me

I'll admit it. I've had a really hard time writing for the last few months. I'm not sure that I'd call it writer's block per se, as that would suggest I didn't have anything to say.

No, by contrast, I've had too much to say - too many feelings, thoughts, insights and memories. I simply haven't been able to wrap my head around them all in order to coherently pare them down to just one topic or specific idea. Nor have I been able to slice through the thick, swirling fog between my ears to be able to find the right words.

And in fact, I still can't. My head and mind and heart are still in such a jumble I don't quite know where to start. But sometimes that is the trick, to *just start.* By getting some of the spinning chaos out of my head and on to paper, perhaps I will eventually sort out what I do want to say and do so in a way which actually is meaningful or helpful to someone besides myself.

The honest truth is, at the moment anyway, it really doesn't matter if my writing helps anyone but me. I am writing for myself, for my sanity, to try and pull back the dark shade of my inner world and let a little light in.

Why the darkness, Sunflower? Why the confusion and overwhelm and lack of words?

It's many things. Some will make sense, others may not.

- The loss of a friend back in the summer. Though Byron was more my husband's friend than mine, his death stirred up so many emotions for me stemming back to my childhood. I identify so deeply with those who are missing him most - it's been gut-wrenching to see them hurting from missing him.

Also, memories and feelings which have stayed dormant for decades have crept back into my daily life and reminded me of lonelier times and what I still miss. Coincidences have linked me back to family who've passed as well as the recently lost friend - a bittersweet reminder that they will never be forgotten but will be out of arms reach as long as I am alive.

- Several amazing opportunities to reconnect with old friends. I've recently visited several dear friends who live far away, which brought me so much joy. Spending time with them and their families truly helped me see love in action and to appreciate my friends for who they are as parents as much as individuals. We laughed a lot and created fun memories.

  Yet as beautiful as our moments were together, the grief I felt upon leaving them was quite deep, and I am bereft facing the idea that I have no idea when I will see them again. Facebook is great but is no substitute for being there.

- Unexpected rifts with family around the holidays. I can't say much on this, but I feel a huge level of being unsettled due to an argument I had around Christmas. My discomfort - and the problems around the incident - has many layers which unfortunately will not likely be smoothed over in the ways they need to be.

  No family is perfect, I know, but with all that is going on at the moment, I really wish mine was just a little more perfect than it is. I have to decide if I let go of some of my deepest truths and beliefs in order to make the peace or if doing so will create a lack of peace inside my heart.

It's a bit of an inner conflict which I'm not sure is better or worse than the family conflict. However, they are both getting to me more than they should.

- A booming, growing, and sometimes needy business. I am truly blessed with an awesome team and learning both to let go and to delegate. This is a huge blessing which took me years to get comfortable with in my first business. Still, I am overwhelmed with all the details and to dos. Doing my best to handle what I must, and trust others can handle the rest.

  I'm also having to face the reality that I can't do everything I want to - at least not at the present moment. I've always been able to juggle a lot of different things and am having a hard time accepting this is changing.

- And of course, the loss and tragedy happening all over the world. From natural disasters like the flooding in Columbia, SC where my best friend lives to the recent terrifying and deadly events in Paris, San Bernadino, Colorado, Lebanon and elsewhere.

  This is probably the biggest thing affecting my overall consciousness. Though I do my best to avoid the news, it is practically impossible to do so, and the overwhelming sadness and negativity just seeps in. I feel like my soul and spirit are being crushed by the meanness and chaos and hate in the world. It's wreaking havoc on every other part of my life and I don't know how or when it will stop.

Bottom line is that I'm overwhelmed, depressed and filled with anxiety. The level of panic and sadness I feel varies from day to day but does not go away.

Some days I wake up wishing I could just stay in bed or that I could run away to a place where there aren't enough people for a terrorist to care about terrorizing - and where I don't have to be an adult. On others, I fantasize about putting myself into a deliciously enjoyable chocolate and zinfandel fueled coma. (Thank God for Xanax and HBO!)

Once I get moving, I am OK for the most part, especially if I have massage clients and other appointments to keep me focused. In fact, once I'm back in my regular routine I'm good until someone starts talking politics or another news flash comes in about the latest event. Then I want to dive back in bed, pull the covers back over my head and pretend it's all a bad dream that will fade away after a nice long nap.

Sigh.

I don't pretend to have all the answers about how to solve the bigger problems of my life or our world. In fact, I have no idea if they can actually be solved. What I know I must do is get out of this murky place of confusion inside my head one step at a time to move back towards a normal inner world. Only then can I reasonably expect to make the outer world a significantly better place.

With that in mind, today I took each task I had to do one at a time and congratulated myself with each new thing I finished. This is what I must continue to do, especially in the areas that support me and my mental health. Some specifics I must do...

- Working out - At least 10 minutes a day (preferably 30) on my bike or the treadmill.

- Eating - 3 healthy meals a day plus snacks. No skipping.

- Water - Drink water throughout the day and before meals. Don't wait until I am thirsty

- Alcohol - Leave it for others as a rule. It can be fun at the time but puts me in a deeper hole. The cost is not worth the reward.

- Rest - Don't over-schedule myself with clients or other work. Allow myself time for fun and to do nothing.

- Vitamins - Take the supplements I know help me *every day*.

Writing this is just for me, but I am grateful to you for being my witness and cheerleader - and perhaps my inspiration. Even those who are used to being the light others look to need to find brighter stars to follow. These words are the beginning of my search for new light. I know something beautiful will illuminate my way back to my true nature and the path of optimism I love very soon.

Let us not curse the darkness. Let us kindle little lights.

Dada Vaswani

All There is IS Love!

"The best place to seek God is in a garden. You can dig for him there."

George Bernard Shaw, The Adventures of the Black Girl in Her Search for God, 1932

My mom was a gardener - an avid one. Today and moving forward, I am choosing to see my mother at her best and happiest, which would likely be in the garden. I'm also sharing the quote above as a step in my own healing and toward repairing my relationship with her. Ditto for the picture as daylilies were her absolute favorite flowers to plant and gaze upon. I hope she likes them both.

It's no secret that my mother and I had issues. I've talked about some of them here and may write a different book exploring them more fully someday. More often though, I tend to keep my thoughts and memories to myself. They've seemed less painful that way.

This year, I've really noticed that my anger with her has crept back up. She's been dead since the summer I was twenty - a suicide - and I've had a long time to deal with my feelings. Thus, I thought I had gotten over her death and all the loss that came before it.

But no... Hiding down in the dark caverns of my psyche I've found drips and drabs of venom and sadness. They'd collected and formed pools of a depth I was shocked to find myself wading in again.

There are so many levels and layers to my anger and sadness - so much yearning for what should have been as well as hurt and resentment for what was there instead. I'm sad for her too because her life could have been so much more rewarding than it was.

Since she left my life the first time and the last time, I've been struggling to peel away and understand all the stratified debris and crap that was piled on during our life/time together. It's gotten heavier with age and has been anything but a life preserver.

Over these last months, well years really, I've paddled and pushed against the heavy currents and undertow which made me feel drowning was almost a foregone conclusion instead of an avoidable accident. I've tried harder to understand her perspective, her history, her limitations, her illnesses.

I've pretended I was fine, ignored the rising waves, and gone out of my way to be sure I was nothing like her. I've literally and figuratively learned how to swim beyond just keeping my head above water; sent out SOS calls for help; and yet I've still been stuck and sinking.

Recently I've called her out and told her she had to let me go, that I was tired of doing things her way, that she had to heal herself and let me move on. I've had numerous healing energy-work sessions which have helped me let go of pieces and parts of our story, but still I've held tight to the idea she was and is not well enough to allow me to go.

But today I had an epiphany.

For the first time I see that MY feelings about her still being sick and damaged are holding HER back. That I am the one who is perpetuating the cycle. Where she is - with God - there is nothing but love. She is still learning, but her spirit and soul have evolved well beyond the limitations of the Earth and what I have placed on her.

By realizing this, I no longer need to have any guilt about achieving or being or having more than she did - or more than she would deem proper - when she was alive. I no longer need to literally work myself into a frenzy trying to earn her love because *all she feels for me now is love.*

And if I do choose to allow my workaholic tendencies to take over my life and schedule, it is perfectly OK for me to be paid for my efforts with money instead wanting or expecting an ethereal nod of approval from her. From her perspective, it's all energy and what is energy if not LOVE?

Admittedly, writing this, I still have some doubts about my unfolding views. But by sharing them, by crystallizing my thoughts on paper, I am able to make them a more solid part of me and to show her that I am finally getting it.

Namaste, Beth, and thank you for helping me to see the truth.

In search of my mother's garden, I found my own.

Alice Walker

Working for Love & Flowers

It's probably obvious I am trying hard to move past some limiting beliefs and emotional pain from the past. Clearly, if you've already read the other stories in this book, you know a lot of my issues have to do with my mother. Plenty of material there, for sure.

One of my other big areas for healing is that of money and prosperity. Money and my mom seem like two different issues, but I am learning just how closely the two are intertwined. And I'm having some pretty big realizations and breakthroughs along the way.

There are SO many stories I could tell about my mom and money to illustrate how my thinking may have gotten a bit screwed up. But for now, let me just say that although my mother grew up in a moderately affluent family, she had a very strong disdain for "people with money." Let's call them PWM for short.

I'm not really sure where Beth's feelings came from. She grew up in an upper-middle class neighborhood in Montclair, NJ, a bedroom community for NYC. Later she went to boarding school before opting not to go to college. Instead, for the most part, my grandparents supported her financially until she married my father - and perhaps even after that.

Whatever the case, while I was growing up, Beth talked about PWM quite negatively. A few examples...

"People with money don't understand what it's like to have real problems."

"PWM don't have any stress."

"PWM didn't earn their money. It was given to them."

And so on.

Though I never ever heard them say anything against PWM, my grandparents, even when they were not hurting for money, were very frugal, and saved EVERYTHING that might possibly be useful at a future time. Having lived through the Depression, they knew what it was like to be People *Without* Money and managed whatever resources they had wisely - other than what they spent supporting their daughter anyway.

They also both espoused the virtues of working hard and persistently to get what you want. They lived by this doctrine and worked a great deal longer than most people of their ages, especially for the time. (My grandfather was nearly eighty-four and my grandmother seventy-seven when they finally retired in 1974.) From them I inherited an incredible work ethic, perhaps one that is a little too good. And from my mother, I got the idea that PWM - even those who work really hard - are bad.

So...my epiphany for today is this: *I've been working against an inner/subconscious belief that I should work really hard to earn my grandparents/others respect, admiration or approval, but not earn much money or else my mother/others won't approve of or love me.*

Wow...just...wow. <u>This explains a lot</u>.

****

In a similar vein, after I wrote *All There is IS Love*, I started thinking about my mother being a gardener. I was comparing the investment she made with her time and energy in creating a garden to the investment I make in my businesses.

In the garden, Beth's labor, talent and love produced an ongoing supply of beautiful flowers, an outward manifestation of all she poured into soil and seed. She could enjoy her beautiful blooms however she wanted without anyone making harsh judgments about her.

She could leave them growing in the ground, cut and display them around the house or give to friends and family. My mom might have even been able to sell or trade some of her gorgeous blooms for other things she wanted if she were so inclined.

Similarly, in my businesses, my labor and talents generate an outward manifestation of my contributions, usually in the form of money. However, given my mom's dislike of PWM, the word and very idea of *money* has often been negatively charged in my life.

At times, it's also been a bit of a challenge for me to manage or even talk about. I now believe her PWM views greatly skewed my thinking as to how to use, share and enjoy money as well how to grow more of it.

But then...da dah...I had another startling revelation!

If ENERGY + EFFORT = FLOWERS for my mom

and

ENERGY + EFFORT = MONEY for my business, then

FLOWERS = MONEY!

What if, when some of my old negative programming comes up related to financial situations, I replaced the word "money" with the word "flowers?" Perhaps this could take away a lot of the icky feelings that popped up and replace them with happy, positive thoughts.

Here's a few I tried out immediately....

"People with flowers don't understand what it's like to have real problems."

"People with flowers don't have any stress."

"People with flowers didn't earn them. They were given to them."

Suddenly, every single one of those statements I've been hearing in my head for decades seemed RIDICULOUS! Since I discovered this new FLOWER POWER, whenever an old money mantra pops into my head, instead making me cringe, I change the words and POOF I start giggling and feeling energized:-)

It's like magic!

The bottom line: I've finally unearthed the roots of some pretty huge weeds in my own garden. I know there's more work to do, but I'm looking forward to planting some new money ideas and manifesting an abundance of beautiful blooms.

Flower power. It does a garden – and bank account – lots of good!

Me in front of my grandparent's old home in Montclair, NJ

Be the Light

It's Christmastime. One of my favorite things about the holiday season is the lights. In an otherwise dark time of year, strands and balls of shimmering color dance around homes and businesses, making what was drab and gray glisten and glimmer.

One of the neighborhoods in our city has turned hanging Christmas lights into an art form, charity fundraiser and athletic event. (Google "Sunset Hills Christmas Balls" to pull up a video and see the difference a little light can make in the world.)

But today I am given the task of spreading my own light with the world. To be clear, today I want to make a difference in someone special's universe, but I'm not quite sure how to do it.

We've had a bit of a fight, one that isn't just fading into the background. Though I can't get into specifics here, suffice it to say a seemingly routine conversation turned heated and harmful quite unexpectedly.

I was very hurt by the other person's words to me, as I believe he was by mine, but I feel even more hurt by the rift that is now growing between us. I don't want our conflict to become one more line on a list of feuds that never got resolved because one or both parties were too proud to make amends. Though it's only been a few weeks, it's time for me to do something to reach out and apologize.

But I'm scared. I'm struggling with what I can say or do to express my sorrow for the argument taking place as well as for my part in it without it being taken wrong.

I don't want it to turn the conversation into another argument or a contest to prove who was right or wrong then or now. I also don't want to come across as weak, whiny or spineless.

What is most important to me is that love is expressed as the primary driver behind what I do/say. The relationship is more important than "being right" about a point of view or opinion. It's OK to agree to disagree.

I have no control of how my words or actions will be taken and am praying for the best outcome possible. I don't know how things will turn out, but I am certain doing nothing to make things right is suffocating my inner spark. If I don't at least TRY and mend the rough edges of this relationship, I will be denying who I really am and darkening the glow of my spirit.

As I continue to seek the right timing and sentiments, I am grateful for the opportunity to reignite what is truly important to me. This holiday conflict certainly illuminated who I really am - including some of my own (usually well-meaning) flaws - and is helping me become a better person and "gift" to those around me. Perhaps the real meaning of the phrase "shedding light" is to look upon the gray areas of ourselves through the gaze of light-filled eyes to see the sparkle that lies (sometimes hidden) in all of us.

May the lights of Christmas and other holidays help you find the sparkle in yourself and others this year and always.

Don't let the insecurities of others dull your sparkle. Shine like the star you are born to be.

Karen Civil

Hope Grows in the Garden

I am not a gardener, well at least not compared to my mother. She, as I have written before, had a passion for plants and an inherent talent in growing them that I do not possess. Granted, I do love flowers, and have spent many happy evenings this spring walking through a local botanical garden with a dear friend.

However, my own garden leaves a lot to be desired - unless you really love weeds. Living in the country, it seems there is a hardier variety of unwanted plants and vines which can take over an entire area overnight. I've gone through fits and starts of trying to tame it over the years, but for the last few I've done next to nothing.

Then recently, I couldn't take it anymore and started ripping out the ivy, mint and other weeds that have overtaken my flower beds yet again. The kid who mows our lawn was due over the weekend and I wanted to feel less embarrassed by the jungle that is my yard.

In doing so, I was thrilled to find a small columbine plant — one of my favorite springtime flowers - was sending up a bud through the thick cover of weeds. This motivated me to carefully clear the area around it, pulling up anything that could threaten its precious existence. Suddenly, I was excited about my garden again and went off to purchase some other flowers to plant.

Imagine my disgust, anger and heartbreak when I got home, and the plant was GONE! Our young landscaper thought he was helping me by weed-eating the previously overgrown flower bed. In doing so, he cut my beautiful baby columbine **TO THE GROUND**. No evidence of it remained other than a few confetti-size pieces of its tender leaves.

That was two and a half weeks ago. Today, my little columbine has rebounded by growing back its' leaves and putting forth a single yet pristine new bud.

Despite being left for dead, the tiny plant came back to life and is doing its very best to live out its botanical destiny. I'm even more excited than before to see that lone little flower open and bloom.

Isn't it amazing how plants will grow in the most unexpected places even after times of struggle and apparent destruction? If this little flower can spring forth with such perfectly beautiful growth - and even produce a flower - after nearly being destroyed, shouldn't people be able to do the same?

The answer of course if yes and no. We can if we simply allow nature to move us forward in the way that was intended. This sometimes means we have to get out of our own way, to break down or move whatever is blocking our light or draining our resources.

As humans we have a tendency to overthink and over analyze every nuance of what knocked our legs out from under us. But using the columbine as an example, I think that the best thing we can do is to just start reaching back towards the light in our lives and stop being afraid to bloom. Do whatever you can to blossom where you are and however you can today. You never know who you might be giving hope to by doing so.

Hope begins in the dark, the stubborn hope that if you just show up and try to do the right thing, the dawn will come. You wait and watch and work: you don't give up.

Anne Lamott

Facebook: Finding the Good in the Bad

Not long ago, a former business colleague who has suffered more than her fair share of difficulties and set-backs of late, was feeling pretty down in the dumps. Why? Facebook!

She recently broke her arm and had to have a pretty extensive surgery to repair the bone. During her recovery, with probably too much time on her hands since she can't engage in many of her normal activities, she's gotten overwhelmed by all the amazing things happening in other people's lives - or at least all the good things they've been sharing on Facebook.

I feel for her, and have had that same experience, both personally and professionally. When your life is feeling pretty sucky, there are some days when the last thing you feel like seeing is how GREAT everyone else's is going! At times like those, all you really want is for someone to show up with a tub or two of Ben & Jerry's and a few hours during which you can commiserate and drown your mutual sorrows by the spoonful.

Still, I want people to share their good stuff online. As I said to my friend, one thing we must remember about Facebook is that some people post only their most exciting things, often glamorizing them to boot - and fail to share the tougher things in life. In a way this is good. There is so much negativity out there, and so much darkness I'd rather know the good stuff.

Yet, when you are hurting, seeing other people's good deeds, happy occasions, and unfailing optimism can only make you feel worse about yourself, like there is something lacking in your own life. But here's the truth...

You are enough just as you are.

Often, when you are willing to share your personal challenges, whether on Facebook, other social media sites, or elsewhere, you can make a HUGE difference just by sharing a piece of a broken heart. By helping even one person, you can change the world.

It may not come with any ice cream but allowing others to see you too have struggles may be exactly what THEY need to get through their own difficult time. It may not be as sweet as two scoops of Rocky Road, but there is a deep level of comfort which comes with knowing you are not alone.

Whatever problems you are going through, Sunflower, you will get through them. Don't be afraid to reach out for support or to tell your story to someone who may need to hear it as much as you need to get it off your chest. It's all good!

You alone are enough.

Oprah Winfrey

Toxic Teachers

Just yesterday I was telling someone how those in our lives who are difficult or cause us pain can actually be teachers. Though this may be hard to see in the best of situations, those we have conflict with often teach us more than anyone else is able. Yet when I am given the "opportunity" to learn from one of my own teachers, I wonder if the lesson is worth the conflict.

What is the difference between someone who is toxic and someone who is a teacher that is difficult? Looking online I came across one article about this issue on SelfGrowth.com by Bill Austin. Though the article - *How to Handle Difficult People: Spiritual Teacher or Downright Toxic* - was helpful, I am still perplexed.

I know we all have stuff to work on. I also know I'm not perfect. But am I as flawed as it appears to this person? Or is he just so consumed with being right - or proving other people wrong - that he will do so at the expense of anyone else's feelings and the relationship between them to do so?

Well, the answer is YES.

The real problem is that I care too much. I care what people think of me. There is nothing that hurts me more than to find out someone I care about has a low opinion of me. I don't want people to think I'm perfect, but I'd like to think I've done enough good in the world to get the benefit of the doubt more often than not.

And yet, I am forced to face the ugly side of myself. I've hurt people too. I've made mistakes, caused conflict and pain in others, put my need for something over the need of preserving someone else's feelings or relationships.

I've taken care of myself at the expense of someone else and spoken negatively behind other's backs. In a way, I am no different from the person who is teaching/hurting me, perhaps other than my intention.

On the other hand, I am trying to heal myself, become better, and make more intelligent choices. I do my best to think before I speak, choose kind words, and stay silent when I am unsure what to do.

From where I sit, my teacher is frozen in a place of anger and bitterness, one that fits him like a glove and insulates him from the risks of being hurt. He pushes people away with his barbs of condescension and spikes of criticism, always walking away the victor instead of the victim.

I am trying so hard to feel compassionately for him and to forgive the words and actions/inactions which have brought about this whirlwind of turmoil inside my head and heart. Yet I am angry and sad that he may never see his way to being or feeling anything but what he is or does now. I thought I was special to him and that the rules which applied to everyone else wouldn't apply to me. Not sure why I thought that way, but I did.

Perhaps this conflict is what I'm using to create "spice" in my life. I've complained a bit lately that my husband is too nice – and he is - and how I am not used to such a smooth ride. Maybe this conflict with someone else is just meant to help me appreciate how lucky I really am.

Whatever the case, for now I choose to learn all I can through this conflict and become BETTER – instead of bitter - from it. If I do feel myself becoming hardened, weaker, or less than I am, I will know the teaching has turned toxic and it is time to step back where I can.

Note: This fight/conflict/feud was deeply troubling to me, so I did a lot of reading to try and help me figure out how to deal with it. I found several others helpful to me in thinking about this situation was on the website, HeySigmund.com.

- *Teaching Kids How to Set & Protect Their Boundaries Against Toxic Behavior*

- *When It's Not You, It's Them: The Toxic People that Ruin Friendships, Families & Relationships*

- *Toxic People*

*****

Several years have passed since I wrote this. I wish I could say time has healed this wound, but it has not, at least not in terms of the conflict. If anything, it's gotten worse to the point where this person and I no longer speak beyond basic pleasantries when forced to be in each other's presence. I've learned that the easiest thing to say to him is nothing, or to simply smile and nod when he is talking and keep my comments to myself unless they are compliments. Of course, this realization only came about after we had another awful explosive confrontation, perhaps worse than the first one.

If healing has occurred, it is in my willingness to let go. I see the situation for what it is and have done my best to stop taking it personally. I think about it a lot less now and have made peace with the idea that our relationship may never be any better. That still saddens me, but it no longer sends me into a dark place. Perhaps one day he'll surprise me, but until then, I do what I need to do to keep my own light burning brightly.

When angry count to ten before you speak. If very angry, count to one hundred.

Thomas Jefferson

The Byron Walk

Dave and I are in the Netherlands to gather with friends and celebrate the life of his best friend, Byron. Last night, we took The Byron Walk, which was a wonderful event and gathering during which we told many stories, shared a lot of laughs and tears, and scattered Byron's ashes over the side of The Kissing Bridge.

The memories from the evening and the rest of the trip to Amsterdam are hard to put into words or pictures well enough to convey properly. But it is clear to me through some specific coincidences that the love and energy Byron brought to life is here with us - in Amsterdam and at home - and carries on though his physical presence is gone.

Here is one: I took the photo of sunflowers early yesterday morning at a local farmer's market which David and I went to with our friend, Neil. Oddly, the photo "disappeared" on my phone and was not in the series of others I had taken at the market.

I had totally forgotten about it totally until I was ready to share pictures from The Onion Soup Party - a much-loved annual tradition with Byron and Dave's friends in Amsterdam - on Facebook. When I opened the gallery on my phone, the sunflower photo from the farmer's market "reappeared" in the middle of the photos taken last night, as if I had shot it during the party.

Perhaps this has no meaning for you or seems to be just a wacky coincidence. But to me it is incredibly moving because of the significance of sunflowers in my life and the healing that they represent. As I mentioned in the story about the dream I had before Byron's memorial service, I've had many experiences in my life of people who have passed on visiting me in my dreams and other ways. To me, this is normal as well as a gift and message.

This whole trip, I've wondered if I might have some type of Byron experience - you know, where I felt his presence stronger than in a typical memory. Since Byron had such a love for technology, it makes perfect sense to me that he would do something with a special photo on my phone to "get my attention" and let me know he was close by.

Though Dave is the person he'd want most to communicate with, I am the one whose connection is more open. Whatever the case, I am deeply moved by this gesture or coincidence and profoundly touched by all the love for Byron I've felt and seen in this city.

I hope all the friends who have gathered continue to share, celebrate and keep the spirit, memory, love and energy of Byron whenever we can, and wherever our travels take us.

How Life Takes Its Shape

"My life takes its shape because of my mother's absence from it."

This line comes from a memoir I just finished reading - *Wishing for Snow* - by Minrose Gwin. Like me, the author grew up with a mother who was less than perfect. Well certainly, most people in the world did not have a perfect mother. But ours were both far less than ideal parents than the norm, in large part because of lifelong mental illness. And both of them are long gone.

Often when someone loses a parent, there are many obvious voids left, and the surviving children pine away, wishing their moms or dads were still around. In every season, countless opportunities, holidays and events unfairly arise, highlighting the lack of presence of their loved one(s), leaving survivors with an intensely painful yearning for their parent to return.

By comparison, it's odd to grieve for a person, especially a parent, whose existence in your life was difficult. Sure, you're faced with the same kinds of events and holidays as everyone else going through a loss, but in many cases your grief is different.

Instead of wishing for Dad to man the grill at your Labor Day cookout or Mom to help with back-to-school shopping like they always did...

Instead of missing their regular phone calls with the latest local gossip or home repair advice...

Instead of craving her famously delicious corn pie and his equally corny jokes...

Those who had difficult parents often miss the people their parents could or should have been. And in some ways, no matter when we lost our parent, we grieved for all we'd lost before they were ever gone.

Grief can be the garden of compassion. If you keep your heart open through everything, your pain can become your greatest ally in your life's search for love and wisdom.

Rumi

Developing Mother-fuck-itude

Not long ago, I read *Wild* by Cheryl Strayed. Though I am not a hiker, I am all about "the journey" and stayed awake well past my bedtime a few too many nights to consume page after page of her misery and wisdom along the Pacific Crest Trail.

With every step she took, I became more invested in and tied to her success, feeling in some ways as I had gone through her pain and trials with her, and even had sore toes. Her writing gave me an extra push to share my own journeys and added a few ideas to the growing bucket list of books I hope to write.

Then this weekend, I attended a writer's conference in which I learned new ways to bring forth my stories and words. I also found myself feeling a little bit of doubt about whether or not I belonged at such a conference with "real" writers.

As I listened to the various experts and editors talk about what makes a good story, a compelling plot, and a strong opening sentence, I wondered if I really have what it takes to make it or if I've just been making a fool of myself by putting out amateurish prose and publishing books which would fail the critical acclaim needed to go big.

Thankfully, a man I really admire, Jeri Rowe, who until a few years ago wrote a regular column in my morning paper, shared this article on Facebook. He may not even know I write, but he knew others needed to see it and I did. In fact, I needed a push to remind me that if writing was easy, everyone would do it. What perfect timing.

The Art of Motherfuckitude: Cheryl Strayed's Advice to an Aspiring Writer on Faith and Humility by Maria Popova

I also thought back to the workshop I took this weekend with Tom Maxwell, formerly of *The Squirrel Nut Zippers*. Tom shared some really interesting perspectives, asides and stories about his life along with some great wisdom:

JUST WRITE. Do it for yourself first - in the spirit of helping others along with yourself. But don't do it so much to impress others or to appeal to a certain audience because you will lose your authenticity. Being truly authentic is more important than pleasing others. Writing is as much about the journey as it is the result that comes from doing it.

I so appreciate the reminders.

After reading Maria's article, and considering also the words of both Tom and Jeri :-), I am not only compelled to finish Cheryl's book - and dig out my SNZ CD - but also to cut myself some slack.

Like many things in life, writing is hard, but in order to get better at it, you must keep writing. If nothing else, I am one who perseveres during tough times to succeed. Often in doing that you learn that you know less than you thought, let go of various preconceived notions, and must reinvent yourself in ways you never expected.

That's what happens as we struggle and cry and let go and heal. New parts of our selves emerge from the fog and fire through the process of never giving up.

So it goes in my writing.

As I struggle to get through adding a few words to the page, I must keep going. Who I am and what I think today may change simply *because* I write. Yet I may have to completely tire one voice or viewpoint for it to die and allow me to find another that is more real and raw.

The important thing is that I write. I must write from **my** heart and express what is in it now, so I can live with myself today, grow into the person I am meant to be tomorrow, and hope my journey, experience and words will speak to and inspire something in yours along the way.

And now I'm off to work on my mother-fuck-itude.

Beauty means expression and being your most authentic self.

Paloma Elsesser

Reject your sense of injury and the injury itself disappears.

Marcus Aurelius

Love Me, Love My Pets

On the first date I had with my husband, David, practically the first topic of conversation was "Love me, love my pets." Running a few minutes late as I dashed in the door of the Thai restaurant where we agreed to meet, I mentioned my dog had delayed my arrival by being uncooperative after our walk.

"Oh, you have a dog," he replied with interest.

Not just a dog. I was coming into the relationship with seven furry friends and knew I might as well breech the subject up front and by telling him the whole story then.

I won't share all their details here, but I guess you could say I am very tender-hearted. All but one of the four dogs (a Lab, a Golden Retriever, a cocker spaniel, and a "Benjy" dog) and three cats (two tortoise-shells, one long haired, one short-haired, and one grey and white tabby) had been rescued from one bad situation or another - and they were my family.

Acceptance of them – and some belief I was not the crazy cat lady - was a must for anyone who wanted to be a part of my life long-term. In other words, my pets were my deal-breaker issue. Thankfully, David took it all in stride, really taking interest in each of their stories, and then told me about his own dog.

After a successful first date, David came to pick me up for a second date several days later. Within moments of his arrival, an immediate bond formed between him and Mojo, my black Lab. It seemed like they were not so much being introduced as they were being reunited. From that day forward, Mojo was a Daddy's boy.

Although it didn't happen quite as fast, David's canine companion, Bart - a friendly Rottweiler mix - in turn became my best friend. Bart was an amiable sidekick who loved to go for rides in my Toyota 4Runner.

Once we lived in the same house, he and I would sneak away for "mommy-doggy" time upstairs, where he would nap on the bed by my feet or somewhere near-by on the floor. He always seemed to know when I was feeling down and would give me extra kisses or untie my shoes to make me laugh. Once, in the midst of an impassioned fight in which I stormed out of the house, Bart forced his way past David to run after me and calm me down.

Thus, I was crushed when Bart was hit by a car. He'd wandered off one night and did not come home before we went to bed. It was raining steadily, darker than normal, and I knew with every passing moment, he was less likely to be OK.

The next morning, a neighbor called to say she found Bart badly hurt on the side of the road just a mile away, but the worst was still to come. The vet could do nothing to help him, and we said goodbye to him that afternoon.

My heart was broken for a long time. Though we still had several other dogs – all of whom I loved – Bart was my baby. He was the one who took care of me when I was feeling sick or sad and was my protector. Yet I failed to keep him out of danger and missed him terribly.

Some months later, my husband came home unexpectedly mid-day. In a huff, he stomped into the house, asking me to come out to the garage. I jumped up, wondering what had happened, and followed him outside. As he pulled open the door to his work van, David suddenly smiled mischievously and said, "Look what I found!"

Inside was a near-perfect carbon copy of Bart David had found abandoned not far from our house. About a year old, the skinny female Rottie mix stood quietly, shyly looking at me from the back of the van through sweet, brown eyes. In an instant, I was in love and cried, "Can we keep her?!"

Though we tried in earnest to find her rightful owners, David and I quickly agreed we had a new dog and my heart began to heal. Because her personality and mannerisms were so reminiscent of Bart's, we decided to call her "Dali Barton" in his honor. However, as few people pronounced "Dali" correctly, her tag now says "Dolly."

Calm, quiet and stoic, Dolly has amazed me with her deep wisdom and grounding presence. Mojo, always the Daddy's boy, hated riding in the car and would panic every time we'd go anywhere. With Dolly there, he would quickly settle down, as if her laid-back attitude rubbed off on him.

When our little dog Brownie (the Benjy dog) died, we took Mojo, Pogo – a beautiful Weimaraner, also found near our house - and Dolly with us to bury her. Pogo, who was Brownie's best buddy, ran circles around the grave, seemingly confused as to why her friend was gone and was freaking out. Mojo, who'd been with Brownie since she was a puppy, turned his back to the grave and would not look at his long-time companion.

But Dolly, in her peaceful, healing manner, walked over to Brownie, took a sniff, and immediately began covering her body with dirt. I wouldn't have believed it if I hadn't seen it myself!

A few years later, when we took Mojo to the vet for the last time, David and I brought Dolly with us, so she would help Mojo stay calm on the ride there. After the visit was over, and we left the vet's office in tears and alone, Dolly was there to remind us life goes on even when we're sad.

Like Bart, Dolly is my dog. Though she was not much of a snuggler when we found her, Dolly now loves to lie next to me on the couch and will often recline across my lap. Sometimes when it's just us at home, she and I, along with Pogo and Buster – a Boxer-Pit mix and our newest rescue - will cuddle together and watch movies all evening. David is always amazed Dolly stays with me so long since she will usually sit with him for a few minutes at most.

Since we got Buster, I've also been impressed with Dolly's abilities as a teacher and pack leader. Though she was not thrilled with the addition of a hyper, testosterone-filled puppy to the household, it became clear early on she would be the one to show him what was allowed and what was not.

At times she will wrestle and roughhouse with him, but Dolly is *always* the one in charge and will emphatically let him know when play time is done. Often, when we take our little pack to the dog park, she will put herself between Buster and whichever dog he is playing with if he takes things a little too far. More than once, I've watched her corral him to the side after he's gotten a bit out of control or tried to run off.

I've loved all our dogs, and know they've loved me, but there's something special between Dolly and me. We seem to have an out of the ordinary level of communication unlike anything I've ever had with a pet.

David often laughs at my assertions that Dolly "tells me things," but she does because she knows I listen. For example, before Buster came along and rightfully claimed the title, David called Dolly "Devil Dog" and she did not like it! She also alerts me with a quick look when Buster is getting on her last nerve and she needs some alone time with me or outside. Likewise, she is the one I turn to when I've had a rough day and my heart needs a little healing.

Dolly is almost nine and I can't imagine my life without her. I know one day, she will tell me without words it's time for me to be the calm one, and to gently move on with my life once she is gone. I dread that day but believe another canine protector will eventually come along to help me heal the same way Dolly did.

Before you get a dog, you can't quite imagine what living with one might be like; afterward, you can't imagine living any other way.

Caroline Knapp

White Heart Healing

Over the weekend, I learned a new meditation. It was part of a continuing education class I took to renew my massage therapy license. In the White Heart Meditation, I was to envision someone who had hurt me or who I needed to forgive. The first person who came to mind was Sam, my father-on-law, with whom I had a huge fight and falling out several years ago.

I closed my eyes, took a few deep breaths, and imagined his face in my mind. As I went through the exercise, tasked with sending a tiny white heart of light and love to him, I saw his face begin to change into one which was sneering, teasing, and taunting me about what a crock this kind of thing is. He laughed at me for my beliefs, practices, and feelings, morphing into a crazy, clownish demon instead of someone who is supposed to – or used to - love me.

Frustrated, I was given the direction to take Sam to an age in my mind where he would be capable of accepting my love and healing. With some effort, I imagined him dropping back from the seventy-two-year-old man he is now to a young adult, then a teenager, then adolescent until he was a young child, perhaps around four or five. This younger version of him was not yet so afraid and hardened by the world around him that he would not accept healing, although he was already quite in need of it.

Next, we were given instructions to see the white heart growing in size and strength. As I watched mine getting bigger, it began to change. First, it folded in half and affixed itself to little Sam's back like a pair of wings on a butterfly. Next it wrapped itself around the top of his shoulders and became a super hero cape that could serve double duty as a shield if needed.

As the heart became bigger, it transformed into a blanket which would keep him warm and dry. Then it became large enough to make into a tent under which he could sleep and rest. Finally, it became the roof of his home and protected him from all the harsh elements outside before covering his whole world.

The meditation ended, and I felt like perhaps I did some good for that little child. I know he and the man he lives inside still suffer from many deep wounds during his childhood. Healing has never been a safe option for him – it is too scary and would cause him to have to face parts of his life and himself he does not want to ever acknowledge again.

I will continue to do this meditation for Sam and send him loving kindness whenever I think of it. Though he may never soften towards me, perhaps he will soften towards himself. I know by tending to his wounded child, I have begun to see him in a new way. Perhaps that is enough for now.

*****

Update…

After the initial session of doing this meditation for my father-in-law, I decided to continue with it as it had helped me feel a little better. Interestingly, each time I have done it, in my mind's eye, Sam has become a little softer and more accepting of the white hearts I send him as well as the idea that a meditation could do either of us any good.

About a week after I started this practice, my husband's parents had an unexpected mini-family reunion at their mountain house near the Blue Ridge Parkway. The reunion, which was sparked by a visit from a cousin who lives in Colorado, filled their house to the brim with overnight guests and mouths to feed.

David, feeling a need to support his parents in hosting the gathering, went up a day earlier than me to visit with his cousins and parents – and be the extra cook in the kitchen. He also did this to provide a buffer so my visit the next day would be as short and painless as possible.

With all the conflict that has occurred between his father and I over the last few years, I was grateful to have the option of arriving late and leaving early to continue westward on a trip to Asheville we already had planned.

I arrived just after noon on a Sunday morning, my beloved niece greeting me in the driveway. She and I made our way inside and I said hello to each of the visiting cousins, my mother-in-law, and David. Within moments, my young nephew got me involved in a game he'd made up rolling rubber balls across the floor and I settled in to the visit.

My father-in-law, Sam, was largely unaware of my arrival as he and the rest of the adult male relatives were hanging around his homemade gun range, showing off their various firearms and proving their manliness. Much of the focus was on my brother-in-law, who was preparing his favorite weapon for a big demonstration before lunch.

On one of his passes through the house to get more ammo or other provisions for the pending "fireworks" display, Sam saw me and exuberantly exclaimed, "Hello Felicia! Welcome!"

Given how distant he's been toward me for the last few years, it was a little odd. I figured he was in an extra good mood since he was getting to show off his shooting skills and gun collection. That was pretty much that, and we didn't speak any more for most of the visit.

But then, after lunch, something really incredible happened. As we were gathering the group for a family picture, Sam called everyone to attention unexpectedly and asked everyone to be quiet.

"Thank you everyone for coming. It is great to have the family together for this weekend. But there is one of our family members who is not here, and who really is having a terrible time."

He was referring to Ashley, one of David's cousins who, in her early thirties, has Stage 3 pancreatic cancer and is losing ground.

"I'm not much of a religious person, but I hear that prayer can work miracles for some people. If anyone needs a miracle right now, it is Ashley. I'd like us all to have a moment of silence and pray together for Ashley."

Then, as my mother-in-law stood beside him with her law trembling and lip quivering, Sam bowed his head and prayed for his great niece to receive a miracle and be healed of her cancer.

I don't remember the exact words that followed, but they were tearful and heart-felt. It was almost surreal to see and hear Sam in this state of benevolence. Then, almost as quickly as it all started, he became his normal gruff self again.

"Ok that's enough," Sam grumbled as he shuffled away from the group and turned off his emotions like a faucet.

I can't tell you how much of a shock this experience was for me, to see this stoic man break down and share a piece of his compassion and vulnerability with his family. I have to believe that the White Heart Meditation had something to do with it.

As we were leaving the gathering, I stopped to give my mother-in-law a hug goodbye. Almost out of nowhere, Sam came into the room and threw his arms around both of us in a hug, thanking me for coming.

Then, once again breaking away from an impromptu emotional interlude, Sam wandered off to get involved in something else as my husband and I collected myself and everything I'd brought so David and I could leave.

The journey is not over, but it is clear some kind of healing has occurred between Sam and I as well as on a number of other levels. It is a step in the right direction, and that IS enough for now.

*When you forgive, you in
no way change the past -
but you sure do change the
future.*

Bernard Meltzer

The White Heart Meditation

Steven Rogat, Shamanic Practitioner, Counselor, and Healer

Used with permission☺

Relax and take some centering breaths. Call in the Light and affirm your willingness to heal a specific situation. Affirm your willingness to communicate with love rather than with anger and/or sadness.

Think of someone you are angry with, someone toward whom you may be holding a grudge, or someone who may be holding a grudge against you. It may be someone with whom you are having a hard time communicating. It could be someone with whom you anticipate having a hard time communicating. Hold a picture of that person in your mind.

Take a few slow, deep breaths, and envision the White Light entering the top of your head, traveling down to the Solar Plexus. On the outbreath, imagine that Light leaving your Solar Plexus. With every breath, you are now breathing Love and Light into your Crown to your Solar Plexus. And you are breathing it out your Solar Plexus...

Send a little white heart out along a cord from your Solar Plexus, and have it enter the other person's Solar Plexus. Keep channeling the Light into your head, through you, and to the other person. This way you are giving that person more than just your own energy. You are giving him a Higher energy. Since you are channeling him the energy, you cannot be drained. You are empowering him AND yourself...

Along that cord, communicate anything you've wanted to, anything that is incomplete or that may have been said before but not listened to. Express it now, but with Love rather than with anger. You can even let him know you are or have been angry with him.

You can tell him you are angry in a loving way, claiming your anger as your own and not projecting blame on him nor anyone else.

You are communicating from your Lower Self to his. See him as a frightened little child. It was his fear that earlier caused him not to listen. It was his fear that made him react with anger and made him wish to inappropriately take control of the situation. Think of how much power he had given away or was robbed of in order to make him want to take power away from others. Forgive that little child.

It is always easier to love and forgive a frightened little child, than it is to forgive an angry, controlling adult.

Send a lot of love to that child. Mentally and emotionally give that child a hug. Let that child hear and accept what you have to say. Review your relationship and see if there is anything else which needs to be said. Send all communications with love. If you can send someone more love and Light than he can send you anger, then you have the situation licked. At least you have done all you could to get back to a harmonious relationship.

Now send him the affirmation that you created earlier. Communicate it in the "I" form. For example, "I now accept response-ability for my feelings, and I allow others to take response-ability for theirs." Send the positive thought along with the appropriate feelings and images. Do it like you mean it!

When complete, while still channeling the Light, see the heart within his Solar Plexus starting to grow. It continues to grow until it totally surrounds him. Still channeling the Light, make the heart brighter and brighter, until there is nothing left but a big, bright heart.

Know that he DID hear what you said. Whether he listens or not is his choice. Know that he DID feel the Love you shared. Whether he acknowledges that feeling or not is his choice, not yours! You have done what you could; the rest is up to him.

Now slowly come out of the meditation (or drift off to sleep if you haven't already), feeling the love, the joy, and the new level of completion you have just given yourself.

*****

Note from Felicia: I usually do this in the morning before I get out of bed. Sometimes I do it for people who need to forgive me as well as those I need to forgive. I also do it or myself as well. I figure we call all use a little more love and forgiveness!

Namaste y'all – and thanks for sharing in this journey with me!

Books, Articles and Resources in Book

BOOKS

You Can Heal Your Life - Louise Hay

Never Quit - Glenn Cunningham

American Miler: The Life & Times of Glenn Cunningham - Paul Keill

Signals: An Inspiring Story of Life After Life - Joel Rothschild

Unfinished Business - James van Praagh

Illusions - Richard Bach

The Witch of Portobello - Paulo Coelho

Wishing for Snow - Minrose Gwin

Wild - Cheryl Strayed

BLOGS & ONLINE ARTICLES

Farewell to my daughter Kate, who died on Christmas Day - Jean Gross
https://www.theguardian.com/lifeandstyle/2015/jan/10/farewell-to-my-daughter-kate-who-died-on-christmas-day

Getting Grief Right – Patrick O'Malley
https://opinionator.blogs.nytimes.com/2015/01/10/getting-grief-right/?_r=0

7 Things Not to Say to a Grieving Person - Katherine Britton
https://www.crosswalk.com/faith/spiritual-life/7-things-not-to-say-to-someone-who-is-grieving.html

Blessingway – What is a Blessingway? - Kelly Winder
https://www.bellybelly.com.au/pregnancy/blessingway-what-is-a-blessingway/#.VJcX8sAAA

Zen Versus Zin – Felicia Brown
www.ZenVersusZin.com

Curves Are Here to Stay - Gazelle Paulo
http://www.theblot.com/curves-are-here-to-stay-7734691

Secrets of Happy People – Dawn Raffel
http://www.oprah.com/spirit/secrets-of-happy-people?FB=fb_omag_secrets_happy_people

Rethinking Mental Illness: Are We Drugging Our Prophets and Healers? –
Fisher Wallace
https://highexistence.com/rethinking-mental-illness-are-we-drugging-our-prophets-and-healers/

How to Handle Difficult People: Spiritual Teacher or Downright Toxic? –
Bill Austin
https://www.selfgrowth.com/articles/how-to-handle-difficult-people-spiritual-teacher-or-downright-toxic

The Art of Motherfuckitude: Cheryl Strayed's Advice to an Aspiring Writer on Faith and Humility - Maria Popova

https://www.brainpickings.org/2015/04/13/cheryl-strayed-write-like-a-motherfucker-advice/

Websites & Other Resources
Tapping with Brad Yates - *http://tapwithbrad.mykajabi.com/*
Whitney Thore
> *TV Show* - *https://www.tlc.com/tv-shows/my-big-fat-fabulous-life/*
> *You Tube* - *https://www.youtube.com/watch?v=Tbcoh5hre74*
> *No Body Shame* - *http://www.nobodyshame.com/*
Zentangle - *Link: https://zentangle.com/*
Ramblin' Rose Events - *http://ramblinroseevents.com/*
Tri for Hospice - *http://triviumracing.com/event/hospicetri2018/*
Sunset Hills Lights - *https://www.youtube.com/watch?v=EkfPlbyNvlA*
HeySigmund.com Articles
> *Teaching Kids How to Set & Protect Their Boundaries Against Toxic Behavior*
> *When It's Not You, It's Them: The Toxic People that Ruin Friendships, Families & Relationships*
> *Toxic People*

Squirrel Nut Zippers - *http://www.snzippers.com/*

Acknowledgements

There are always so many people to thank at the end of a large project like this. It is almost impossible to remember them all, but I always feel the need to express gratitude.

Thank you first of all to *everyone* who has inspired these writings, from the authors and writers whose work sparked an idea in me, to the many teachers in my life who help me learn in so many ways.

Thank you to all who are a part of my family, whether we are bonded by blood, marriage, friendship, our journeys, or some other way. I am lucky to have such a large community of people who care about me so much.

Thank you to everyone who has read my work and provided me with feedback or comments about how it touched you and how it could be better.

Thank you to the many "angels" in my life who help me find and follow the light I might have been unaware of. You may not realize how your stories, observations and words of wisdom have helped me gain insight, understanding and inner peace.

In particular, I thank those who have read or listened with care to these stories before they became a part of this book. In particular, thank you to Nancy Triplett and Carol Brown for your willingness to read the early drafts of this compilation.

Thank you to my husband, David. Your level of steady commitment to me and our relationship is unlike anything I've ever experienced. You have provided a safe place for me to heal from many wounds as well as to explore the deeper meaning of so many events and memories. Thank you for accepting me with all my quirks, demands and needs. You are a great husband and awesome doggie daddy ☺

Gratitude to everyone else who has helped me with my writing, this project, and my life in general, especially those who have taken time to teach, nurture, mother, mentor and/or love me over my lifetime.

In no particular order: Maxine Brown, Marcia Kass, Peggy Norvell, Lisa Oshust Harryman, Barbara Oshust, Mary Jo Bullins, Betty Salter, Joan Thain, Mary Hudspeth (& Oma), Pedie Shore, Karen (Karine) Webb, Kay Phelps, Glo Cunningham, Whitney, Cathy Jordan, Lucy Wellmaker, Sharon Swift, Susan Huber, Liz Price, Michelle Kammerdiener King, Phyllis Ingold, Beth & Sam Clayton, Mary Gold, Bart Kincaid & Tim Taylor, Angie Dubis, Tammy Moody, Leslie Young, Lessie Everton, Judy Glasgow & Irwin Smallwood, Janice Smith, Teresa Fisher, Rhonda Wilson, Joanna & Jesse Godwin, Bill & Alex Dove, John & Gloria Dove; Ellen Dove & Louise Sparkman; Suzanne Dove-Garcia, Kiki Jamieson-Dove and all my Dove cousins, Tina & Shad Allen, Seymour & Carol Levin, my Book Club girls (especially Paula Morrow!), my massage school class mates from CSMT, my incredible team at A to Zen Massage as well as all the amazing massage therapists, estheticians and other service and spa providers educators, professionals and clients who have worked with me through the years, and of course all my loving dog and cat babies and companions. I am grateful for you all!

Made in the USA
Columbia, SC
10 November 2018